# Monitoring & Auditing Practices
# for Effective Compliance

# Contributors

Annette G. Barreau, JD
Broad and Cassel
Fort Lauderdale, FL

Thomas Boyle, JD
Buchanan Ingersoll PC
Pittsburgh, PA

Gregory A. Brodek, JD
Duane Morris LLP
Bangor, ME

Katherine A. Lauer, JD
Latham & Watkins
San Diego, CA

Susan Lemanski, JD
Ernst & Young
Washington, DC

Emmy S. Monahan, JD, LLM
Duane Morris LLP
Bangor, ME

Jan Murray, JD
Squires Sanders LLP
Cleveland, OH

Lester J. Perling, JD
Broad and Cassel
Fort Lauderdale, FL

Alan Peterson
Tucker Alan Inc.
Chicago, IL

Robert Ramsey, JD
Buchanan Ingersoll PC
Pittsburgh, PA

Dorothy Regas Richards, JD
Squires Sanders LLP
Cleveland, OH

David Rowan, JD
Squire Sanders LLP
Cleveland, OH

Catherine Sreckovich
Tucker Alan Inc.
Chicago, IL

Ronald L. Wisor, JD
Arent Fox
Washington, DC

# Monitoring & Auditing Practices for Effective Compliance

**Edited by**

## John E. Steiner, Jr., JD

**Chief Compliance Officer**
**Cleveland Clinic Health System, Cleveland, Ohio**

**With 14 contributors**

Health Care Compliance Association
Philadelphia, Pennsylvania

10  9  8  7  6  5  4  3  2  1
ISBN # 0-9713156-1-2

This publication is designed to provide accurate and authoritative information in regard to the subject matter covered. It
is sold with the understanding that neither the authors nor
the publisher are engaged in rendering legal, accounting or
other professional services. If legal advice or other expert
assistance is required, the services of a competent professional person should be sought (from a Declaration of Principles
jointly adopted by a Committee of the American Bar
Association and a Committee of Publishers).

To order copies of this publication contact

HEALTH CARE COMPLIANCE ASSOCIATION
1211 Locust St.
Philadelphia, PA 19107

Telephone: 888.580.8373
Fax: 215.545.8107
Email: info@hcca-info.org

Quantity discounts are available.

# Contents

# Foreword

Maybe Socrates was a compliance officer. Wasn't it Socrates who said the unexamined compliance program isn't worth having? Maybe that is a bit far-fetched, but my point is that evaluation and assessment—monitoring and auditing—are hardly new concepts. Good health care organizations have been doing regular self-evaluations all along. And most health care organizations have regular inspection through the Joint Commission or other accreditation bodies. So why is a book on monitoring and auditing so important?

Compliance programs have made great progress in the past three years. The 1999 HCCA Profile of Health Care Compliance Officers found the greatest goal for compliance programs in the coming three years would be program development and implementation. Monitoring and auditing was identified as a goal too, but only 41% saw it as a top goal for the coming three years.

Compare that with the 2000 HCCA Profile of Health Care Compliance Officers when 88% of respondents—more than twice as many as the year before—identified monitoring and auditing as a top goal in the coming three years. Things changed dramatically in just one year. While the most recent survey, the 2001 HCAA Profile of Health Care Compliance Officers, identifies the introduction of HIPAA Privacy Regulations as the important new challenge on the horizon, fully 83% of 2001 respondents still identify monitoring and auditing as a top goal for the coming three years. And 50% of respondents to the 2001 survey identified monitoring and auditing as the biggest issue facing their program today. Again, only HIPAA Privacy Regulations ranked higher. As compliance programs have become established, compliance officers no longer need to worry as much about program development and implementation issues. New regulations will always be a challenge, but the issue of monitoring and auditing remains a major ongoing concern for compliance officers today.

Federal Sentencing Guidelines released in 1991 identify "implementation of auditing, monitoring and reporting systems to ensure and foster compliance" as an essential element of an effective compliance program. The 1998 Office of Inspector General Compliance Program Guidance for Hospitals is organized around these Federal Sentencing Guidelines, and noted prominently in the Guidance is the need for a system for auditing and monitoring: "An ongoing evaluation process is critical to a successful compliance program." It should be noted too that every Corporate Integrity Agreement requires the organization to perform regular monitoring and auditing at least annually. While the directive may sound clear enough, how, who, and what to monitor or assess are not so easily determined. Even after how, who, and what have been determined, there are still innumerable details and seemingly unending questions of interpretation to be addressed. It is no wonder monitoring and auditing remain high on the list of big goals and major issues.

John Steiner has brought together a stellar team of compliance consultants and health care attorneys from around the country to address key topics related to monitoring and auditing. These experts are affiliated with prestigious firms and are dealing directly with the daily challenges of monitoring and auditing in healthcare. The result is *Monitoring & Auditing Practices for Effective Compliance*. This important book addresses the hot topics that are making monitoring and auditing such a concern.

In the 2001 Profile, auditing was identified by the Chief Compliance Officer (CCO) respondents in survey results as the second most important industry experience needed by a

CCO. Commonly, CCOs have to develop this skill or externally provide on-the-job training for themselves and others in the organization. *Monitoring & Auditing Practices for Effective Compliance* will be a valuable tool to assist in this training and development.

Not that long ago, developing and implementing compliance programs were daunting challenges. Since 1999 the percentage of health care organizations with active compliance programs in place has increased from 55% to 80%. Compliance programs must be nurtured and maintained, fostered and protected. They must be monitored and audited. *Monitoring & Auditing Practices for Effective Compliance* provides a useful tool for compliance officers who recognize monitoring and auditing will continue to be a major focus for organizations in their compliance programs and related efforts. This book will be critical for compliance officers who care about the details of monitoring and auditing and want to get it right.

Maybe Socrates was a compliance officer ahead of his time. I won't comment on whether the unexamined life is or isn't worth living. But certainly, the "unexamined" compliance program is looking for trouble. *Monitoring & Auditing Practices for Effective Compliance* is available as a resource to assist you with necessary examinations.

We at HCCA are pleased to provide this book for our members and we hope you find it helpful. Please feel free to contact us with feedback on this book as well as ideas and suggestions for future ones. We welcome your input.

**Sheryl Vacca**
*Director, Deloitte and Touche*
*Health Care Regulatory Consulting Practice*
*2002 President, Health Care Compliance Association*

# Preface

*Monitoring & Auditing Practices for Effective Compliance* was prepared to assist compliance officers and members of compliance committees with the monitoring and auditing tasks associated with designing and maintaining an effective corporate compliance program. The book is based on my experience in compliance and on a realization that, since the late 1990s, corporate compliance in the health care industry has evolved to the point where continuous monitoring and auditing steps should be commonplace.

Experiences of other regulated industries with corporate compliance reflect a 10-year evolution from early efforts to resist government enforcement actions (usually through a combination of legislative advocacy and litigation) to reluctant acceptance of additional or new internal controls through either voluntary or mandatory compliance programs, and finally to acceptance and repetition of compliance monitoring and auditing steps.

At this point in the evolution of health care compliance programs, a basic structure should be in place, and appropriate employees should be receiving training and education on substantive risk areas, as well as instruction on their delegated compliance responsibilities. What may be lacking, and what this book addresses, is sustained attention to monitoring and auditing practices for effective compliance.

The management of this project was assumed by Nancy Puckett of HCCA and the copy-editing services of Tracy Mastro of Ernst & Young were generously provided. Those efforts are gratefully acknowledged.

*John E. Steiner, Jr., JD*

# Introduction

The articles in this book provide practical guidance and advice from a diverse group of practitioners with a unifying theme: basic auditing and monitoring practices to sustain compliance activities. These practices are especially relevant for health care organizations to understand and apply to *voluntary* compliance programs because, failing voluntary efforts, those same practices likely will be applicable to *mandatory* compliance programs. Since "forewarned is forearmed," this book presents topical guidance for use in voluntary compliance programs to help the reader anticipate what may be imposed involuntarily, if voluntary efforts are either nonexistent or deemed inadequate. This book is divided into three parts.

**Part 1, Basic Compliance Monitoring and Auditing Issues,** consists of four main topics with contributions from members of law firms and consulting firms. The basic components of effective compliance can be depicted as a continuous cycle with four key steps—assess, plan, implement, monitor—involving diverse personnel and resources in each step.

Chapter 1, *Developing an Effective Compliance Team,* addresses the cultural, political, and practical issues that are critical for identifying the right personnel and approach for sound compliance programs. The authors have extensive expertise in many regulated industries, including health care.

Chapter 2, *Using Statistical Sampling to Challenge Overpayments and Assess Compliance Audits,* is a must read for understanding statistical principles applied to compliance issues. The author has successfully defended clients at the earliest stages of investigations and prosecutions by methodically analyzing and challenging the use of those principles by regulatory agencies.

Chapter 3, *Retrospective Versus Contemporaneous Reviews,* co-authored by health care attorneys with a broad health care client base, gives thoughtful and thorough treatment to a difficult issue that arises in all compliance investigations—retrospective and prospective reviews. While there are no easy or straightforward answers to those issues, the authors present certain conventional wisdoms.

Chapter 4, *The Attorney-Client Privilege in the Context of Health Care Compliance Investigations,* is also authored by attorneys with a large health care practice and condenses the many important topics and points related to this relationship in a straightforward fashion.

**Part II, Voluntary Compliance Monitoring and Auditing.** This section is slightly less structured than Parts I or III, in part because a "voluntary" compliance program is supposed to be tailored to the organization's unique needs and resources. As noted by the OIG in the *Model Voluntary Compliance Guidance for Hospitals,* "an effective program should incorporate thorough monitoring of its implementation and ongoing evaluation process." The auditing and monitoring portion of the Guidance provides "at a minimum, these audits should be designed to address the hospital's compliance with laws governing kickback arrangements, the physician self-referred prohibition . . ." The Guidance also states, "An effective compliance program should also incorporate periodic (at least annual) reviews of whether the program's compliance elements have been satisfied. This process will verify actual conformance by all departments with the compliance program."

Chapter 5, *Financial Relationships With Physicians: Auditing and Monitoring Anti-Kickback Statute and Stark Law Compliance,* addresses the power of health care professionals to refer or order, which is a central theme in health care that directly affects how most health care funds are spent. This theme and the underlying laws that address concerns with that power are discussed by a health care lawyer. In short, a voluntary compliance program should include this topic on its must-do list of monitoring and auditing tasks.

Chapter 6, *Developing a Voluntary Disclosure and Refund*, co-authored by individuals with substantial experience with defense procurement fraud matters and voluntary refund protocols, presents insightful advice and tips on this topic. In most cases, the critical aspects of how well a voluntary compliance program was designed and implemented are revealed through the process of making a voluntary refund. The OIG states that one measure of effectiveness is whether and how often the organization makes refunds. Thus, refunds are a predictable result of ongoing monitoring and auditing steps.

Chapter 7, *Medicaid Program Provider Self-Audits*, covers an aspect of health care compliance that often arises with the Medicaid program. Medicaid is an important area of focus in any compliance program and the steps implemented by state programs to address perceived health care fraud and abuse are presented here, along with advice for dealing with audits.

**Part III, Mandatory Compliance Monitoring and Auditing.** This section should not be necessary for organizations that have developed sound voluntary compliance programs or successfully defended themselves in investigations or prosecutions. Nonetheless, since no one can be 100% compliant or predict future risks that might materialize in their organizations, there remains the possibility that mandatory compliance programs, with their reliance on Corporate Integrity Agreements and Independent Review Organizations, will be imposed on an organization. The authors of the topics in Part III address the practical issues and suggest techniques to deal with mandatory compliance program issues.

Chapter 8, *Corporate Integrity Agreement Negotiations*, written by a health care lawyer, is a must read to help you plan your voluntary compliance efforts and be prepared if a mandatory compliance program is inevitable.

Chapter 9, *Preparing for an Independent Review Organization Engagement*, describes practical insights and experiences from the perspective of a large firm that serves as an IRO. This chapter addresses key issues that an organization needs to consider when conducting business under the terms of an externally imposed compliance program.

Every attempt has been made to include current, substantive material on each topic. However, neither the Editor nor the Publisher can warrant the accuracy of the content of each topic. Competent, professional advice should be sought in any compliance matter that may involve the reader or his or her organization.

# Basic Compliance Monitoring and Auditing Issues

# Developing an Effective Compliance Team

## Alan Peterson and Catherine Sreckovich

B y now, it is clear that the United States government is seeking to change the corporate conduct of health care organizations by issuing regulations and guidance that encourage the health care industry to adopt a new and better model of self-governance and corporate compliance.[1] This is occurring largely because there is a direct correlation between an industry's acceptance of, and reliance on, federal funds (e.g., Medicare reimbursement) and the amount of government scrutiny, expectations and demands for regulatory compliance with new and existing rules and regulations.

The increased scrutiny and demand for regulatory compliance necessitate stepped-up self-governance on the part of health care providers.[2] Enhanced self-governance motivates and protects many entities, including government entities such as the Department of Health and Human Services' Centers for Medicare and Medicaid Services (formerly the Health Care Financing Administration) and Office of Inspector General, the Department of Justice, Congress, and health care providers, insurers and fiscal intermediaries.

However, improving self-governance usually requires considerable change. An organization working to achieve effective and sound change needs to do so with great care.[3]

---

1. Although this chapter focuses its attention on health care providers, the principles and recommendations summarized here are believed to have broader application.

2. This is a common regulatory development. The authors refer interested parties to the United States public utility, defense, telecommunications and railroad industries. What is often overlooked is a key reason for the stepped-up self-governance: The industry fears greater government regulation will result in significantly greater inefficiency, a weaker health care system, poor service and higher costs. In other words, private participation—or a joint public-private solution—is better.

3. As to the often-asked question—"Can an industry, such as health care, avoid greater regulation at a time of increased federal support?"—the short answer is "No." The reason is what is known as the Golden Rule: "Whoever has the gold makes the rules." With greater reliance on government reimbursement comes more government regulation. In the long run, regulation can be eased but rarely is it totally eliminated.

Changes in governance require changes at a variety of levels, including corporate policy, corporate organization and personnel.

First, the highest echelons of management, that is, the Board of Directors and the most senior executives, must generate and support new policies requiring greater self-governance and internal compliance. Second, a health care organization must effectively and appropriately develop its corporate organizational structure for self-governance, and this structure must support the organization's policies and procedures. And, third, it is wise for an organization to establish a new or improved compliance team that is responsible for effecting change and that has a direct reporting relationship to the Board and senior executives.[4]

There are many important factors to consider when forming or enhancing a compliance team. This chapter describes some of these factors and briefly explains their significance.

Compliance generalities notwithstanding, it is the authors' recommendation that the compliance function within a health care organization report both to senior management and the Board of Directors. This reporting relationship can set the tone for the organization's desired level of commitment to compliance (i.e., it demonstrates the organization is serious about compliance). Moreover, both management and the Board should receive reports on a regular basis that discuss the progress being made, as well as challenges being faced, by the compliance function. While this approach will not guarantee success, it is a strong step in the right direction.

The level of commitment of the Chief Compliance Officer and compliance team depends on the size of the organization and the challenges the organization faces. A larger organization may have a full-time Chief Compliance Officer, while a full-time position may not be feasible or essential for a smaller organization. Full-time commitment from a Chief Compliance Officer, however, can serve as a signal to regulatory agencies that the organization takes the matter of compliance seriously.

Moreover, senior management support of the compliance program is more likely if the organization makes certain that:[5]

1. The Compliance Officer is someone who the Chief Executive Officer, the Chief Financial Officer and the Chief Operating Officer trust implicitly.
2. The Chief Compliance Officer serves as the balance between the Chief Financial Officer and the Chief Operating Officer, on behalf of the Chief Executive Officer, on compliance matters. Moreover, a Chief Compliance Officer must be able to work effectively with the senior management team, the Board of Directors and others within the organization.
3. Senior management is given the time it needs to read and understand the compliance information provided by the Chief Compliance Officer and the compliance team.
4. Senior management is aware of the importance of compliance and program elements such as billing corrections, voluntary self-disclosures and voluntary refunds.
5. Senior management has the time and other resources necessary to promote and carry out compliance improvements.

---

4. The government often requires this direct reporting relationship to the Board and senior management.

5. These are generalizations designed to focus organizations on key requirements important to the success of the compliance team. The titles used here may not be the same as those used in some organizations.

6. The Board of Directors takes the time necessary to learn about compliance in general, and about any existing allegations of noncompliance within the organization—especially any involving fraud and abuse—so they may make informed recommendations regarding noncompliance issues and provide policy support for organizational compliance.[6, 7]

An organization's compliance team—from top to bottom—must be a reasonably cohesive unit that works well together to make sure as little falls through the proverbial "cracks" as is possible. A compliance team is also responsible for making sure the entire health care organization is up-to-date on the state of the regulatory environment. In addition, the dynamic nature of today's health care regulatory environment suggests that a competent, flexible and adaptable compliance team is essential to promote the success of a health care entity's corporate compliance program. Assembling an effective compliance team, however, can be a challenging process.

## Make the Chief Compliance Officer Part of the Senior Management Team

An important first step in creating a compliance team, or improving the effectiveness of an existing one, is to place the Chief Compliance Officer on the organization's senior management team, so the Chief Compliance Officer reports directly to the Chief Executive Officer or his or her counterpart.

It is important that an organization conduct a thorough search for its Chief Compliance Officer, including consideration of both internal and external candidates. This person should be well versed in good business practices, health care regulations specific to the organization and, if possible, the company's current operations. It is preferable—although not always possible—that the Chief Compliance Officer have prior experience with the compliance function; areas of knowledge might include billing, billing adjustments, voluntary disclosures and refunds, system improvements and training.[8]

The Chief Compliance Officer should also be a leader who is skilled at helping the organization identify existing and potential compliance problems, and remedying or avoiding such problems. It may be difficult to find an individual with strong leadership skills; in the long run, however, the absence of these skills will be a hindrance to

---

6. For a similar grouping, see *Report on Medicare Compliance*, "When a Compliance Program Is a Sham: One Chief Compliance Officer's Nightmare and How to Avoid It," Atlantic Information Services, Inc., November 16, 2000, p. 3.

7. The Board of Directors should be acutely aware of compliance activities and should ask questions of the compliance team. In addition, the Board should be informed about what the Chief Compliance Officer is doing and how the Chief Executive Officer is responding to the findings of the compliance plan. The Board should make sure the organization's senior leaders see to it that resources are in place for activities such as corrective actions and training. The Board's active involvement will help the organization maintain an effective compliance program.

8. While the Chief Compliance Officer position does not necessarily require the technical or clinical skills such as those possessed by an MD or RN, such skills can be valuable.  Moreover, it would be wrong to assume that a technically trained person should not be a Chief Compliance Officer, or to require the Chief Compliance Officer to be, for example, a financial person.

anyone in this position attempting to handle the organization's internal and external matters.

The level of corporate employee serving as Chief Compliance Officer can be a factor in internal organizational decisions as well as external matters. For example, in matters involving the federal government, the organization usually is better off having a Chief Compliance Officer who is high-level in the organization. The Department of Justice considers involvement of upper-level management in compliance to be more significant than involvement of lower-level employees.[9] If an organization becomes involved in a voluntary disclosure or questionable compliance situation, the federal government will take into consideration the organizational level of the Chief Compliance Officer. In particular, if the Chief Compliance Officer has the ear of the Chief Executive Officer, the government will most likely view this favorably and note this fact in its analysis and evaluation of the compliance situation.

Some health care organizations may be tempted to look to the organization's Internal Audit group for compliance leadership personnel. Based on the authors' experience, it is generally not a good idea to move an employee from the Internal Audit department into the role of Chief Compliance Officer.[10] Although Internal Audit employees may have reasonable knowledge of the company's procedures and practices, and may even have some audit and review skills, they often lack operations skills and leadership experience.[11, 12] An effective Chief Compliance Officer must be able to demonstrate leadership skills and have operational knowledge of the organization.

Regardless of the size of the health care organization, the Chief Compliance Officer should be a proven leader who will command the respect of all internal line and staff departments. This individual should also have the authority and influence to involve the senior management team as necessary when there is a compliance concern within the organization—preferably before the compliance concern becomes a serious or pervasive problem.

The Chief Compliance Officer must wear many different "hats" in his or her role. He or she has to work well with internal organizational groups including the legal, operating and financial departments, as well as with the organization's Board of Directors and Chief Executive Officer. The Compliance Officer also has to work effectively and have credibility with external entities such as carriers, fiscal intermediaries and regulators.

Many health care organizations experience internal conflicts between various departments and the Chief Compliance Officer.[13] For example, if the Billing Department's policies are different from Internal Audit's policies regarding compliance, and the Chief Compliance Officer does not have the mandate in the organization to set the standards for com-

---

9. Many of the views summarized in this document were shared by the authors with the health care industry on two separate occasions: the first in a presentation to the Association of American Medical Colleges, September 24–26, 1997; the second in a presentation to The Minnesota Hospital and Health Care Partnership, November 3, 2000, at the University of Minnesota.

10. The Internal Audit department does have leaders, but generally speaking, has few personnel to spare.

11. Here "operations skills" means pricing, providing health care services, negotiating, anticipating compliance risks, etc.

12. Current organizational thought believes compliance to be an area requiring specialized training and, more significantly, a totally independent function within the organization. If the compliance function is considered to be too "close" to Internal Audit, it could jeopardize the perception of its total independence.

13. It is a fact that the turnover among Chief Compliance Officers is quite high.

pliance policies, the compliance program can be seriously compromised. Compliance programs must provide the Chief Compliance Officer with the authority to reconcile, standardize where appropriate and sometimes modify policies that cut across departmental organization lines. Conflicts between groups or departmental functions with vastly differing policies and procedures may render a compliance program virtually ineffective.

## Ensure the Compliance Officer Has the Requisite Skills

When conducting a search for a Chief Compliance Officer, there is another essential factor to consider: This individual must have the requisite skills to help design, implement and monitor an effective compliance program for the organization. To be successful, the candidate, first and foremost, must be a leader. If possible, the Compliance Officer candidate should not only be a leader in the general sense, but a leader in the health care field as well. Since health care compliance is a relatively new area, it may be difficult to find a candidate with both health care and compliance knowledge and experience.[14] In any case, he or she should fully appreciate the importance of compliance in general, the unique nature of billing corrections, disclosure refunds, and system and practice changes.

A top quality Chief Compliance Officer will already have a good deal of experience in, and an extensive understanding of, the way the company or provider unit does business; if not, he or she should be able to quickly gain that understanding. The best compliance officers, to date, have been people who lead by reason and logic, personal strength and a strong sense of fairness.

An organization should also assess candidates for the Chief Compliance Officer position based on the quality of their decisions and ability to demonstrate sound judgment.[15] The Chief Compliance Officer should be able to follow the company's compliance plan and not veer from it for any reason. This person will be required to make sound decisions in haste and under pressure. He or she will have to be able to carefully analyze and consider the relevant factors of a procedural change or voluntary disclosure situation. The candidate will also have to be a leader for the organization in an emergency and very high-pressure situations. As a result, leadership and decision-making skills are very important.

It is also helpful if the Chief Compliance Officer has the ability to anticipate new risk areas to avoid future compliance problems.[16] In addition, some knowledge of statistical

---

14.  It is fair to say that demonstrated leadership in compliance and experience in health care would "tax the available pool of leaders too much in today's health care facts and circumstances." Health care compliance has only been a high priority focus in the last few years. Practically speaking, people with experience in both health care and compliance are difficult to find. It may be necessary to get the best person and train that person up by way of competent outsider help and inside organizational assistance.

15.  Although a somewhat redundant assertion here, a strong Chief Compliance Officer will have an understanding of, and appreciation for, dealing with complex and sometimes ambiguous regulations.

16  For a brief peek into the United States General Accounting Office's (GAO) views of how the Centers for Medicare and Medicaid Services must not only improve its regulatory efforts, but also develop better regulatory oversight, see "Medicare Improper Payments: While Enhancements Hold Promise for Measuring Potential Fraud and Abuse, Challenges Remain," United States General Accounting Office Report to Congressional Requestors, September, 2000.

sampling is necessary, particularly in areas such as understanding the strengths and weaknesses of various sampling methodologies, interpreting sampling results and communicating information about sampling in simple terms.[17] Finally, it is helpful for the candidate to have some systems and control knowledge and experience, since much of the data used by providers, insurers and intermediaries is systems based and since use of that data with reasonable assurance must rely on the systems and controls.

## Build a Team That Can Manage and Maintain the Compliance Program

When an organization is considering whether or not to implement or enhance its compliance program, it should consider this: If convicted of improprieties, a health care organization will have a compliance program imposed upon it, which will probably be far more costly and onerous than the one it develops voluntarily.

Some organizations may decide to hire outside consultants to help them develop their compliance programs. These consultants usually have extensive experience developing compliance programs and are knowledgeable about the intricacies of the health care industry. Consultants also serve to supplement otherwise scarce internal health care compliance resources.

Consultants and other subcontractors for compliance may report to the Chief Compliance Officer; some of them, however, may report directly to outside Counsel to protect confidentiality and the attorney-client privilege. Eventually, the compliance team should have sufficient resources to maintain an effective compliance program, with consultants serving as a resource as necessary.

## Consider the Costs-Benefits Ratio of a Compliance Program

Maintaining an effective health care compliance program is an expensive endeavor; the costs of compliance are often difficult to estimate and hard to recover. However, an organization should evaluate the costs of an effective compliance program against the less tangible—although quite possibly substantial—costs of billing adjustments, disclosures and voluntary refunds as well as other intangibles such as loss of reputation and market share.[18] The costs of not having an effective compliance program or not having one at all are much higher than having one. It took defense contractors and the Department of Defense a long time to finally accept the fact that the cost of compliance is simply a cost of doing business in today's environment—this will undoubtedly be true for the health care industry as well.

---

[16 continues] This report discusses the direction the GAO recommends the Health Care Financing Administration should proceed regarding federal payments, what health care Chief Compliance Officers may be facing in the future, and some interesting background and more current developments.

17. If the Chief Compliance Officer does not possess this statistical knowledge, it is important that he or she seek outside support in this area.

18. Here "the market" means the customers, funding or reimbursement sources, the securities markets for publicly held securities, etc.

## Conduct Periodic Evaluations of the Compliance Program

One major assignment of the compliance team is to audit and monitor compliance program activities. The purpose of these activities is to ensure the program is operating effectively. The objectives of testing and evaluating the compliance program, however, must be clear; clear, testing objectives can be a means to improving quality and operations within the organization.[19] In other words, it is not enough to have a compliance plan; it must be audited and monitored on an ongoing basis so any vulnerability in the program can be identified and fixed. Testing the compliance program provides assurance that the relevant constituencies—the senior management team and Board of Directors, operating departments and groups delivering the health care services—are aware of the risk areas that require priority attention. Auditing and monitoring can also identify new risk areas so the organization can take action before errors occur or become pervasive.

The United States government has displayed interest in internal evaluations of compliance programs. For example, the Federal Sentencing Guidelines call for the use of monitoring and auditing systems: "The organization must have taken reasonable steps to achieve compliance with standards, by utilizing monitoring and auditing systems reasonably designed to detect criminal conduct by its employees and other agents."

Some organizations form compliance committees, which meet regularly to review compliance standards and discuss potential improvements to the compliance program. The success of such committees, however, is highly dependent on the level of key line and staff members' attendance and the company policy on dedication to compliance. Relevant compliance committee members often are representatives of the compliance function and include senior management, operating departments and human resources representatives plus internal Counsel. When these groups meet and work well, they make a real contribution to compliance goals.

## Implement Strong Training as Part of the Compliance Team's Development

An organization's strength can be significantly aided by sound training. So it is in health care compliance. Such compliance training is a sacrifice as well as another form of investment—a health care investment that may pay high dividends and one that certainly will help avoid compliance problems.

Compliance training requires capable health care leadership. It is noteworthy that experienced compliance health care personnel can do, and want to do, what is called "double duty" as trainers and line performers. All that is needed is leadership, guidance, encouragement and reasonable support resources.[20]

---

19. Not only is this "clear objectives" requirement important for the goal of achieving compliance, it is even more significant for the efficient delivery of health care services.

20. Training in health care compliance need not be unduly expensive. Indeed, such health care training can be Spartan.  Health care personnel appreciate training and respond to that training very effectively.

## Conclusion

If an organization were to contrast its own internal auditing today with 15 and 30 years ago, or contrast similarly the general internal auditing in the United States with that of 15 and 30 years ago, vast changes would be observed. It would be seen that such changes included higher level reporting, far-reaching revisions to the scope and character of audit or review work performed, better leadership, stronger personnel in general, more valued skills involved, and on and on about strengthening and improvement.

By thinking in terms of that internal audit analogy—a very real one—organizations can often see emerging compliance needs as a desirable step in their own big picture.[21]

There are challenges to the development of an effective compliance team. For example, there are certain key traits that must be embodied by the individual who is selected to serve as the Chief Compliance Officer. Although a qualified Chief Compliance Officer may be difficult to find, much of the success of a corporate compliance program rests on the leadership skills of this person. The Chief Compliance Officer and an effective compliance team are key to a compliance program's success and ultimate effectiveness.

*The views presented are based on the authors' experiences as consultants to the health care industry; neither Catherine Sreckovich nor Alan Peterson is an attorney.*

---

21. For two versions of excellent text on internal controls and auditing, see Richard L. Ratliff, Wanda Wallace, Glenn Sumners, et al., *Internal Auditing Principles and Techniques* (2nd ed.), The Institute of Internal Auditors: Altamonte Springs, FL, 1996.

# CHAPTER 2

# Using Statistical Sampling to Challenge Medicare Overpayments and Assess Compliance Efforts

## Lester J. Perling and Annette G. Barreau

I n recent years, the Centers for Medicare and Medicaid Services (CMS, formerly the Health Care Financing Administration or HCFA), through its Part A intermediaries and Part B carriers (the Contractors), has taken an aggressive stance in audit and post-payment reviews of Medicare providers' and suppliers' claims. This increased activity has resulted in increased overpayment assessments.

The vast majority of the Contractor audits do not involve review of 100% of the claims submitted by the target provider or supplier. In most cases, only a sample of claims is reviewed, as determined by statistical sampling. Statistical sampling is the process through which a sample of a defined population is studied to determine the characteristics of that population. A sample can be representative of the population from which it is drawn if the sample is randomly selected and sufficiently large. The results of the study of the sample are used to make assumptions about the population from which it is drawn; this process is known as "extrapolation." According to a long-standing HCFA (now CMS) ruling, sampling has a presumption of validity as to the amount of an overpayment that may be used as the basis for recoupment.[1]

It is recommended that health care providers use statistical sampling in auditing as part of their own compliance efforts to determine whether they are complying with applicable laws and regulations, or to determine if the federal government has overpaid them. It is also usually required as part of the audit process for certain health care providers that are under government-mandated corporate integrity agreements (CIAs). In addition, the government uses statistical sampling to assess penalties against providers that have violated Medicare program requirements.

Statistical sampling is generally considered appropriate if an objective sample can be drawn and the sample is based upon a randomly selected and statistically significant number of sample claims. A 100% review of the claims will result in a cost disproportionate to the amount that can probably be recovered, or such review is otherwise impractical.

---

1. HCFA Ruling 86-1

Sampling is not an appropriate method for estimating overpayments made to individual beneficiaries,[2] for items that involve large sums of money (assuming that the number of claims is manageable)[3] or for a small number of claims.[4]

Although the Medicare program uses statistical sampling to determine overpayments and encourages its use by providers and suppliers to make their own overpayment assessments, the sampling study must be performed correctly. A Contractor's failure to perform a sampling study correctly is one of the most effective arguments to challenge an overpayment determination or the calculation of penalties. If successful in an overpayment challenge, the amount of the overpayment is reduced to the amount of reimbursement the provider received for the services in the sample that remain denied after all appeals are completed. This usually results in a significant percentage reduction in the overpayment amount. Moreover, even if the provider does not have a good argument to challenge the substantive basis for the overpayment (e.g., lack of medical necessity or documentation, a challenge to the statistical sampling procedures is still available).

## Use of Statistical Sampling Other Than in Projecting Overpayments

If a provider desires to perform a statistical sampling of its own claims for purposes of assessing a possible overpayment it has discovered, the Office of Inspector General (OIG) of the Department of Health and Human Services does not allow the provider much freedom regarding how to perform the study. The OIG has published specific guidelines in the *Provider Self-Disclosure Protocol* ("Protocol")[5] that Medicare providers must follow when they use statistical studies to quantify overpayments they identify through their own internal compliance efforts and are disclosing through the Protocol.[6] The OIG encourages providers to "police themselves, correct underlying problems and work with the Government to resolve [potentially fraudulent] matters" through voluntary self-disclosure. As part of the Protocol, the OIG directs the provider to assess the monetary impact of the disclosed matter. In making such an assessment, the OIG specifically approves the use of statistical sampling. Although the OIG is not obligated to accept the results, substantial weight will be given to results that follow the Protocol. The OIG's recommended procedures may also be used in other voluntary forms of overpayment disclosure, such as to Contractors and the Department of Justice.

The self-assessment plan should identify the objective of the review, the population group (also called the "frame"), the methodology used in selecting the population, the source of the information for selecting the population and the qualifications of the personnel involved in the process. The plan should also identify the elements that comprise the population and the sampling frame. Documentation should be included that discusses how the audit sample differs from the sampling frame, and any effect this difference has on the conclusions reached as a result of the audit.

---

2. Medicare Carrier's Manual (MCM) §§ 7151, 7154(A)

3. MCM § 7153

4. MCM § 7154(B)

5. 63 Fed. Reg. 58399 (Oct. 30, 1998)

6. *Id.*

The Protocol contains a number of specific requirements for self-assessment studies. The sample must be designed to generate an estimate with at least a 90% level of confidence and a precision of 25%. The final sample size should be determined through the use of a "probe" sample. (A probe sample is a small probationary sample used to measure the characteristics of the population being studied and determine an appropriate sample size.) There must be a minimum of 30 randomly selected units in the probe sample, which may not be used as part of the full sample. Random selection must be utilized in selecting all samples; a simple random sampling may be used unless the provider documents a need for a more complex method. (A simple random sample is one in which every member of the population has an equal chance of being selected as a part of the sample and the population is not divided into distinct subparts—e.g., outpatient vs. inpatient). The characteristics used for testing each sample should also be identified.

As noted above, the OIG requires the use of sampling in most of its CIAs. A recently published document, "Frequently Asked Questions Related to OIG Corporate Integrity Agreements," offers additional explanation about why the OIG supports the use of probe samples. In that publication, the OIG states:

> A probe sample, of at least 30 sampling units, should be examined. The units for the probe sample should be randomly selected using a random number generator. . . . Results from the probe sample allow the reviewer to make estimates about the overpayments in the population. As a result, the reviewer can estimate how many sampling units will need to be reviewed to achieve certain confidence and precision levels. A 90% confidence and 25% precision level is required in current CIAs [Corporate Integrity Agreements].

Clearly, the OIG views probe samples with at least 30 randomly selected units as statistically valid for determining the appropriate number of sampling units to be used in an actual statistical study. If a provider does not use a probe sample that contains at least 30 sampling units, the OIG will not accept the provider's ultimate statistical results. Interestingly, neither the OIG nor the Contractors regularly use probe samples to determine the correct sample size in their studies.

The OIG has also published a series of model compliance guidances (Guidances) for a variety of health care providers, institutions and suppliers.[7] In each guidance, the OIG requires providers to monitor the effectiveness of their compliance programs. A recommended monitoring technique involves sampling protocols that allow the organization or practitioner to identify and review variations in performance from an established baseline.

In the Guidance for durable medical equipment, prosthetic and orthotic suppliers (DMEPOS),[8] for example, the OIG recommends that all DMEPOS, regardless of size, conduct audits to ensure compliance with the applicable statutes, regulations and policies. However, the OIG recognizes that the small DMEPOS may not have the resources to audit its operations to the extent suggested in the Guidance. At a minimum, the OIG recommends that the small DMEPOS conduct an internal audit using the OIG's Audit Manual to

---

7. The OIG has published Guidances for hospitals, home health agencies, nursing facilities, hospices, durable medical equipment, prosthetics, orthotics and supply industry (DMEPOS), third-party medical billing companies, clinical laboratories, Medicare choice organizations, and individual and small physician group practices. All Guidances can be found on the OIG Web site at http://www.dhhs.gov/oig.

8. OIG's *Compliance Program Guidance for the Durable Medical Equipment, Prosthetics, Orthotics and Supply Industry* (June 1999: http://www.dhhs.gov/oig/modcomp/cpgfin.htm).

help design it. The DMEPOS may choose to review a random sample of claims based on the risk areas it identifies and conduct an initial baseline audit, and then periodically conduct follow-up audits. Also, the DMEPOS should document the results of all audits it conducts.

Similarly, the OIG recommends that third-party medical billing companies that create a compliance program incorporate periodic compliance audits, which may be conducted by internal or external auditors. The review process should include presentation of written evaluative reports on compliance activities to the governing body of the company. According to the OIG, the evaluative reports should include a valid statistical sample of claims submitted to federal health care programs.[9]

In the recently published *Guidance for Individual and Small Group Physician Practices*,[10] the OIG recommends that practices conduct periodic audits by randomly selecting a number of medical records. Recognizing that small practices have limited resources, the OIG does not create a set formula on how many records to review, but states that five or more medical records per federal payor, or five to ten medical records per physician, would be acceptable. The OIG also states that larger sample sizes will produce more accurate results and recommends that, at a minimum, a practice should conduct a review of claims that have been reimbursed by federal health care programs.

The government uses statistical sampling to assess civil monetary penalties (CMPs) and determine exclusions from the Medicare and Medicaid programs. A CMP may be assessed for each claim that constitutes a violation of the statutes governing the Medicare and Medicaid programs. As a result, the potential exists for a substantial CMP depending upon the number of violative claims. The government bears the burden to prove that the claims violate the rules governing the Medicare and Medicaid programs.[11] In doing so, the government may introduce the results of statistical sampling, if based upon an appropriate sampling and computed by valid statistical methods, as evidence of the number and amount of claims.[12] The results constitute evidence of the number and amount of claims and, if the government has made out a *prima facie* case, the burden then shifts to the respondent to "produce evidence reasonably calculated to rebut the findings of the statistical sampling study."

## Challenging Statistical Sampling Procedures

There are various publications that contain varying requirements for the use of statistical sampling in overpayment determinations. *The Medicare Carriers Manual* (MCM), the *Medicare Intermediary Manual* (MIM), the OIG's *Audit Manual*, CMS's (formerly HCFA's) *Program Integrity Manual* and *State Medicaid Manual* (Program Manuals) as well as HCFA rulings, have established guidelines that must be followed when using statistical sampling. Furthermore, on January 8, 2001, HCFA published a *Program Memorandum*

---

9. OIG's *Compliance Guidance for Third-Party Medical Billing Companies* (November 1998: http://www.dhhs.gov/oig/modcomp/cpgfin.htm)

10. OIG's *Compliance Guidance for Individual and Small Group Physician Practices* (November 2000: http://www.dhhs.gov/oig/modcomp/cpgfin.htm)

11. 42 C.F.R. §§ 402.19, 1005.15

12. 42 C.F.R. §§ 402.109, 1003.133(a)

(Memorandum)[13] regarding use of statistical sampling that became effective immediately and replaced the *Medicare Carriers Manual Sampling Guidelines Appendix* (the Appendix); this change affects all overpayment audits conducted by Medicare Part B Carriers. The Memorandum significantly reduced the requirements that Carriers had to follow. In fact, the Memorandum states that "[n]othing in these instructions precludes [HCFA] or you [i.e., the Carrier] from relying on statistically valid audit sampling methodologies employed by other audit organizations . . . and other authoritative sources." These provisions appear to give the Carrier significant latitude in conducting its audits when using statistical sampling.

Further, the Memorandum states that if a sampling study has certain characteristics, then "assertions that the sample and its resulting estimates are 'not statistically valid' cannot legitimately be made. In other words, a probability sample and its results are always 'valid.'" This is an assertion with which many statisticians would probably disagree, and it is one that will certainly be litigated extensively in coming years as Carriers begin to utilize the Memorandum to support their sampling studies. The Memorandum does state that the sample design must be "properly executed." This is an important point that will have to be addressed in future litigation regarding this Memorandum.

Nonetheless, in order to be performed correctly, the sampling study must be consistent both with program requirements as set forth in the Program Manuals and with, what is sometimes called, generally accepted statistical procedures (GASP). Failure to follow these requirements renders the statistical study invalid and results in violation of the provider's constitutional right to due process. If government agencies fail to follow their own policies, the result of the sampling study cannot be used. Consequently, the requirements set forth in the various governing Program Manuals and GASP become the fodder used to challenge the government's sampling study.

## Documentation

There are several areas in which the government most often falls short in its statistical sampling studies; perhaps the most frequently occurring of these shortfalls is the government's maintenance of required documentation. The Program Manuals require that documentation be provided, and the Appendix is, perhaps, the most specific about this. In particular, the methods of sampling and extrapolation must be fully documented so that others can perform a post-audit review to verify the Appendix requirements have been met and the study is valid. Required documentation includes the frame (the population), the method of randomization (how the random numbers were generated and how the starting point was obtained) and the method of extrapolation. If this documentation is not provided, then it is impossible to replicate the study or to perform a post-audit review. In such cases it would be difficult to determine the credibility of the results. GASP requires that results must never be accepted on blind faith, but rather on the basis of careful audits of the data and procedures used.

Documentation is also required for all computer programs used in the sampling study for extrapolation and for statistical analyses. Without them it would again be difficult to determine the credibility of the results. It does not follow that calculations and analyses are correct simply because a computer performed them. Computer software should not be presumed to be perfect since it could have flaws. There could be mistakes, for example, in

---

13. HCFA Pub. 60B, *Program Memorandum, Use of Statistical Sampling for Overpayment Estimation When Performing Administrative Reviews of Part B Carriers*, January 8, 2001

the computer program itself or in its execution, which could produce faulty outcomes and biases in the results. Programming errors, in particular, can lead to serious flaws in both the sample and the extrapolation. The results do not reveal flaws because it is often the case that apparently random outcomes are, in fact, not random. Unless a computer program is verified through audit, there is no way to certify that the sample generated is "representative" and that the extrapolation is "statistically significant."

The HCFA Memorandum significantly reduces the amount of documentation required for Carriers, although it still requires that the Carriers provide complete documentation of the sampling methodology they followed. The documentation required is the most basic documentation that would be expected in any type of sampling study.

The Program Manuals, GASP and the Memorandum all require that sufficient documentation be maintained to allow for verification and replication of the study. This documentation is necessary to prove, among other things, that the sample was randomly selected—this is perhaps the most critical element in ensuring the validity of a sampling study. To be statistically valid, the sample must be selected at random, with no biases or other distortions that could make it not "representative." Sampling that specifically omits low charge claims, for example, would not yield a representative sample. Also, there should be adequate documentation to support the assertion that a random sample was, in fact, selected.

Often there is no documentation or even any indication as to how exactly the sample was drawn. In such cases there is no proof that it is a scientifically valid, randomly selected sample with a population of elements that had an equal probability of being selected. If no documentation is provided about how the sample was drawn, then the study cannot be replicated and its results cannot be audited or verified. More often than not, government agencies fail to either retain the required documentation or, if they do, do not make it available to the provider during the appeal, thus making it impossible for the provider to assess or replicate the study. Consequently, as part of an appeal of any overpayment that is determined based on a sampling study, the provider should request a copy of all documentation required to be maintained by the Program Manuals and GASP. If key documents are not produced, that alone could be sufficient for the extrapolation to be overturned. In fact, this argument has been successfully used in a number of recent cases.

For example, in a recent decision by the Medicare Appeals Council (MAC) of the Departmental Appeals Board of the Department of Health and Human Services, the MAC overturned an extrapolated overpayment of several million dollars because of the Medicare carrier's failure to provide critical documentation to the provider, thereby violating the provider's right to due process.[14] Similarly, several administrative law judges (ALJ) have overturned extrapolated overpayments because of the government agency's failure to maintain or supply critical required documentation. In one very recent case, the OIG had deleted the frame from its computers, and the ALJ overturned the extrapolated overpayment.[15] Other ALJs have made similar rulings. Some of these will be discussed in more detail.

## Sample Size

Another requirement that Contractors often fail to meet is the selection of a sufficiently large sample to ensure that it is representative of the universe from which it is being

---

14. In re Physicians' Affiliated Services, Inc. (August 10, 1999; DAB Decision)
15. American Health Care Services (Hon. J. McAfee) (February 23, 2000)

drawn. The sample size, that is, the number of claims in the sample, must be large enough to ensure "statistical significance." The Appendix provides a minimum required "Basic Sample Size," depending on the expected overpayment and whether or not the sample is stratified. Frequently the sample size is too small or even inappropriate because it is not consistent with the Program Manual requirements.

The Memorandum, on the other hand, does not have a specific sample size requirement, but does concede that the size of the sample "will have a direct bearing on the precision of the estimated overpayment. . . ." The Memorandum states it is not possible to specify a minimum sample size that applies to all situations. It seems to be trying to send a message to administrative review bodies by stating that "[a] challenge to the validity of the sample that is sometimes made is that the particular sample size is too small to yield many full results. Such a challenge is without merit as it fails to take into account all of the other factors that are involved in the sample design."

Contractors sometimes use a standard computer program to select sample size. This program automatically uses a sample size of 30, regardless of the amount of the expected overpayment, which is not consistent with basic statistical principles that call for a method that reflects the specific situation. For an expected overpayment in excess of $25,000 with a nonstratified sample, for instance, the Appendix requires a sample size of 320. A sample size of 30 under these circumstances is not justified, either in terms of the numbers of beneficiaries or in terms of the size of the total charges and the expected overpayment. Such small sample sizes are also inconsistent with GASP, and the deviation from both the HCFA requirements and GASP is typically not explained. Furthermore, a small sample size is inadequate to ensure the sampling error is kept within bounds.

It is inappropriate to choose a sample size using a "one-size-fits-all" approach because it may result in a sample that is neither "representative" nor "scientifically valid." It is analogous to everyone wearing the same size shoe, which works for some people but does not work for most. Typically, Contractors do not conduct pretesting or take probe samples to determine the appropriate sample size based on the variability in the population. The Memorandum does not even mention testing, unlike the Program Manuals. Pretesting involves some initial sampling to determine if the sample size and method used for selection did indeed provide a statistically valid sample. Without such pretesting, the appropriate sample size tends to be a "guesstimate" for which there is no valid justification, particularly when a sample is chosen arbitrarily and independently of the specifics of the situation under study, such as in the use of a standard computer routine. Formulae are readily available to perform this type of sample size estimation; the Appendix contains one such formula.

The Program Manuals and GASP contain methods by which a proper sample size can be determined, but these are rarely used. Instead, government agencies arbitrarily pick a sample size and use that for all of their studies. For example, the OIG and Medicare intermediaries generally choose a sample size of 100, the minimum size allowed by their respective manuals.[16] Often, intermediaries do not even use this minimum. Even the CMS Administrator has criticized a sample size of 100 as not being large enough to justify recouping large overpayment amounts.[17]

---

16.  MIM § 3940.3C; OIG Audit Manual § 20-06-50

17.  Memorandum from Associate Regional Administrator, Division of Financial Management, to Michelle Snyder, Acting Director, Office of Financial Management, *New Part A Provider Audit Sampling* (February 1, 1999).

## Sample Stratification

A third major area of possible error is improper stratification. Stratification is the process whereby a sample is subdivided into groups containing similar members when the universe contains dissimilar members. Each stratum is separately studied and a separate error rate is established for each, which is then applied to the universe. This is necessary when the universe contains significantly disparate reimbursement amounts or other characteristics (e.g., inpatients and outpatients). Once again, the Program Manuals and GASP all require that samples be stratified in certain situations. Failure to do so, or even doing so when it is not appropriate, can skew the results and, therefore, invalidate the sampling study. Although the Memorandum encourages stratification when there is a reasonable basis for grouping the sampling units, the Memorandum states incorrectly that failure to stratify does not invalidate the sample or bias the results.

As mentioned, when the population is stratified, it is divided into different sub-populations that are relatively homogenous even when the overall population is heterogeneous. Simple random sampling is then performed over each of the strata. Stratification, when used correctly, can result in a greater precision than nonstratified sampling. The stratification method selected must be appropriate to the population in question and its use should be justifiable. It also must be based on some real differences that caused the need for stratification in the first place. For example, consideration should be given to the type of health care service being analyzed. Hospital services might be stratified into inpatient, outpatient and other such categories, while physician services might be stratified by diagnostic categories. Total charges can also be a valid basis for stratification. Some computer routines always stratify by total charges, and typically subdivide data into five strata. This approach does not make sense because the number of strata used is arbitrarily selected: that is, there is no reason for choosing five strata, rather than, say, three or eight. This approach also lowers the effective sample size to six for each of the five strata, so that the resulting estimates can be significantly affected by the presence of one outlier. Typically, there is no pretesting or pilot study conducted to determine the appropriate way to stratify the population, if at all.

Contractors do not often use stratification despite a heterogeneous population. This is like adding the proverbial apples and oranges, and the results can be as nonsensical. In these cases, stratification should be done according to the categories that led to heterogeneity in the first place. Conversely, sometimes stratification is used despite a population that is homogeneous. This is the case with certain computer software that automatically stratifies data. In this case the effect of stratification is to reduce the sample size considerably to the numbers chosen in each stratum.

In a recent case in which a Medicare Part B Hearing Officer overturned an extrapolated overpayment, the universe contained services reimbursed at either approximately $1,000 or $4,000. The sample contained primarily the higher reimbursed service, although the universe contained more of the lower cost service, thus skewing the overpayment upward. Stratification, in conjunction with a larger sample, would have prevented this problem.

## Relative Error

There is a method of measuring the variability of the units in a sample, known as the "relative error rate" (which is also another term for "coefficient of variation"). The higher the relative error rate, the less representative the sample is of the universe from which it is drawn. The Appendix states that the relative error rate for any sampling process should never exceed 12 percent. One expert statistician, who serves as a consultant for a Contractor, issued a memorandum to that Contractor that stated the "target is to get a coefficient of variation of no more than 5% in large claims and 10% in small claims," with "small" defined as $5,000 or less. The statistician also indicated that a coefficient of variation greater than 10% is not acceptable. Attacking a sampling study based on a high relative error rate has proven effective in some cases.

A flaw of the relative error method is the potential appearance of unrepresentative outliers in the sample. The presence of such outliers can create a bias in the sample, shifting upward the level of estimated overpayment. Choosing elements that are not representative can lead to a sample that is not "representative" and an extrapolation that is not "statistically significant."

Even though the other possible flaws in statistical studies, such as outliers, have not proven to be the most successfully argued during appeals, all flaws should be raised on appeal, since it is impossible to predict which issue will be considered significant to those reviewing the overpayment assessment. Although there are other possible flaws in statistical studies, the four flaws discussed above have proven to be the most successfully argued during appeals of overpayments.

## Guidance After a Sampling Methodology Is Ruled Invalid

The Memorandum includes a section entitled "changes resulting from appeals," which instructs the Carriers what to do if a court rules the sampling methodology is invalid. First, if the decision issued permits the correction of errors in the sampling methodology, then the overpayment should be revised after the corrections are made. This requires consultation with CMS's regional and central offices to make sure the revisions are consistent with the administrative or court decision. Second, the Carrier may elect to recover only the actual overpayment related to the sample claims (currently the most frequent choice among Carriers). Finally, the Carrier may conduct a new review for the sample time period and forego recovery of any overpayment remaining from the initial review. It is also important to note that any studies performed during the time frame in which the Appendix was in force should still be reviewed and challenged, if appropriate, based on its requirements and not the looser requirements of the Memorandum.

## Federal Case Law Addressing Statistical Issues

A review of the federal case law addressing statistical sampling reveals that it is the general policy of the courts to give auditing agencies great deference in the method of statistical sampling used by them to project overpayments. Many providers have argued that the use of sampling deprives them of their constitutional rights—specifically, their due process rights. Providers have attempted to argue that before the government can take away their property or right to compensation through use of sampling, they have a protected right to require Medicare to review each claim independently. However, courts have consistently held that Medicare may use statistical sampling to project overpayments, thus creating a rebuttable presumption of an overpayment with the onus on the provider to demonstrate the inaccuracies in the sampling method or size. The rationale the court sets forth for allowing statistical extrapolations of overpayment claims is centered around balancing the administrative burden of the government versus the provider's interest in the fairness and accuracy of the statistical sampling. The federal courts have held that the government's interest in administrative efficiency outweighs any interest of the provider.

In *Ratanasen v. California Dept. of Health Serv.*, CCH 42,040, No. 91-16786 (9th Cir. 1993), the court ruled that the use of statistical sampling in determining overpayments is proper and in compliance with the law, provided the party being audited is given the opportunity to rebut the audit results. Statistical sampling was determined not to be a violation of procedural due process rights because the provider can provide evidence to contradict any disputed results of the audit, allowing the provider a fair recourse. The court noted that to deny agencies the use of such methods would be to deny them an effective means of detecting abuses in the use of public funds.

Similarly, in *Chaves County Home Health v. Sullivan*, 931 F.2d 914, Medicare & Medicaid Guide (CCH) & 39 (D.C. Cir. 1991), *cert. denied*, 502 U.S. 1092 (1992), the court found that statistical sampling adequately protects the provider's interests and right to appeal because the provider could appeal any specific claim in the sample or the sampling procedure as a whole. This ability to appeal any specific claim ensured protection of the provider's procedural due process rights under the Constitution. Further, the burden on the government interest would be too onerous if it had to review 100 percent of the claims in the population being audited. The court noted that the sampling must be made from a representative sample and must be statistically significant to be valid.[18]

The provider in *Yorktown Medical Laboratory, Inc. v. Perales*, CCH 39,672 (2d Cir. 1991), who was assessed an overpayment, unsuccessfully argued that he was denied his right to payment for clinical laboratory services. The court found that the provider's claim failed because he did not have a property interest in the payment, nor did he have a legitimate entitlement claim in the payments that were withheld. In order for the provider to succeed under a due process argument, he must challenge the findings that he misused Medicaid billing codes.

Providers have also claimed that the methods used in auditing were flawed and unfair, and that the burden should not fall on the provider to prove that the auditing methods were flawed. Rather, providers have argued that government agencies should have to prove their procedures were valid. The federal courts have disagreed, however, and have consistently held that the burden is on the provider to demonstrate flaws in an auditing agency's sampling method.

The court considered this issue in *Illinois Physicians Union v. Miller*, 675 F.2d 151 (7th Cir. 1982), when the plaintiff brought an action challenging the procedures used by the Illinois Department of Public Aid (Department) to audit physicians who are reimbursed for their medical services under the Medicaid program. The court determined that the issue was whether the state, in attempting to preserve its welfare monies, could place the burden on the individual physician to demonstrate that the Department's calculations were inaccurate. The court noted that, at all times, the burden is on the physician to prove entitlement to welfare monies.

The court held that the use of statistical sampling to audit claims and arrive at a rebuttable initial decision as to the amount of overpayment was reasonable where the number of claims rendered a claim-by-claim review a practical impossibility and the physician is provided with an adequate opportunity to rebut the determination. The court offered a number of methods a physician may use to rebut the Department's calculations. The physician may present evidence that: (1) there were errors made in reviewing the actual cases making up the sample pool, (2) cases that were not reviewed but make up a portion of the universe of cases for the assessment of overpayment were medically necessary and

---

18. See also *Mile High Therapy Centers, Inc. v. Bowen*, 735 F. Supp. 984 (D. Co. 1988).

reasonable, (3) the methods used to compute the overpayment were inaccurate or (4) that waiver of liability should apply.[19]

Providers have also challenged the validity of the statistical sampling methodology. In *Daytona Beach General Hospital, Inc. v. Weinberger*, 435 F. Supp. 891 (M.D. Fla. 1977), for example, the plaintiff hospital contested the use of statistical sampling in determining Medicare overpayments when the sample was based on less than 10 percent of the total cases in question. The court held that the use of such a small sample size denied the plaintiff due process.[20]

In making these challenges, it is important to present supporting evidence at all levels of the appeal process. The plaintiff in *Webb v. Shalala*, CCH 300, 330 No. 98-3075 (N.D. AK. 1999), failed to show that he presented evidence at the ALJ hearing that proved the statistical sampling was flawed. The physician in this case argued that the statistical sampling method used by the Carrier to project the amount of the overpayments was invalid. In particular, the physician was concerned with the size of the sample and the validity of the calculations of the overpayment.

The court rejected the physician's argument that the statistical analysis was flawed. The court noted that the record failed to show evidence that the statistical sampling was flawed. Further, the court concluded that although Dr. Webb made the base assertion that the sample size was so small its use to arrive at a large assessment deprived him of his right to have each individual case examined and to protest the assessment, it was clear that Dr. Webb had the opportunity to challenge the audit method and had access to an appeals procedure.

---

## Administrative Law Judge and Departmental Appeals Board Decisions

Challenges to statistical sampling methods have been far more frequent at the administrative level. Providers are often successful when it can be shown that: (1) the administrative agency has failed to adequately document its sampling methods (thereby making it impossible to re-create the sample to challenge its accuracy), (2) the size of the sample is insufficient to ensure its accuracy, (3) the auditor has failed to follow the procedure set forth in the relevant Program Manual, (4) the relative error is too large to ensure fairness and accuracy or (5) the prosecuting party has failed to offer evidence as to the validity of the sampling in question.

Many of these challenges were successfully made in *American Health Care Services* (American), February 23, 2000. In that case, the OIG conducted a statistical sampling of American's 1993 claims and concluded that American had been overpaid. American challenged the overpayment determination as a violation of its due process rights. In particular, American argued that: (1) the government failed to accurately document sampling procedures and perform sampling techniques as required by the OIG's Audit Manual, (2) the

---

19.  See also *State of Georgia v. Califano*, 446 F. Supp. 404 (N.D. Ga. 1977); *Mercy Hospital v. New York State Dept. of Social Services* (App. Ct. 1992) (holding that the state does not have to show that the provider's records are inadequate to conduct a case-by-case review).

20.  See also *Mount Sinai Medical Center of Greater Miami v. Mathews*, 425 F. Supp. 5 (S.D. Fla. 1976). (The court held due process concerns require that the government's representations of the procedure it has utilized in determining overpayments be accurate and correct.)

OIG did not use an adequate sample size, and due process requires that a sample size be adequate in order to support extrapolation and reliability, (3) the government should have performed a stratified sampling instead of an unstratified sampling and (4) the relative error rate exceeded acceptable limits.

The ALJ found that American was not liable for the overpayment at issue because the overpayment was based on an invalid statistical methodology, which amounted to a depravation of American's constitutional right of due process because of the inadequacy of the sample size and the high relative error rate. The ALJ further noted that the government portrayed a "cavalier attitude about 'living with the precision' that a sample of 100 gave them with apparently little regard for the consequences to the provider." Finally, the ALJ stated that the government's actions were arbitrary, capricious and egregious in its sampling procedure.

HCFA requested a review of the *American* decision to the MAC. The MAC found that the ALJ's decision was correct and that the government's statistical methodology used to assess the overpayment was a depravation of procedural due process.

The ALJ, in *Morrow Skin Clinic and David M. Morrow, M.D., Inc.*, December 30, 1994, discussed the importance of following the Appendix. The ALJ "conclude[d] that the guidelines in the Appendix are identified as a minimum standard for conducting a reliable sampling.[21] As such, a sampling, which falls below the standard, will not be considered reliable." The ALJ specifically found that a sample size was inadequate, the stratification was invalid and that "improper reliance was placed on a small number of inadequately selected cases from that sample." The ALJ concluded that the methodology used to project the overpayment at issue was "not statistically valid and, therefore, the total overpayment was incorrectly extrapolated."

Providers have invalidated statistical sampling methods used by Contractors due to the Carrier's failure to maintain documentation required by the Appendix. For example, in *Dr. Glenn H. Osterweil, DPM*, September 24, 1999, a podiatrist argued that the statistical procedures used in the overpayment determination were inconsistent with HCFA requirements, not statistically valid and fundamentally unfair, thereby rendering them arbitrary and capricious. The podiatrist further contended that the Carrier failed to follow the minimum standards for the sample size, noting that the adequacy of the sample size can be measured by the relative error, which will tell the investigator whether the sample size is sufficiently large to give valid results. The ALJ found that the Carrier did not maintain the required documentation and that the Carrier did not follow Appendix guidelines.

Similarly, in *Physicians Affiliated Services, Inc. (PASI)*, March 26, 1997, the MAC concluded that the appellant made a valid challenge to the statistical methodology because there was no list of the universe or documentation to support the sampling methodology in the record. The statistical extrapolation of the overpayment was set aside, consistent with the requirements of due process stated in HCFA 86-1.

Other providers have challenged a Contractor's failure to select an adequate sample size. For instance, the provider in *MK Diabetic Support Services*, September 17, 1998, argued that the statistical samples used by the government to extrapolate an overpayment were invalid because the basic sample size of 320, with a stratified sample and an expected overpayment in excess of $25,000, was inadequate.

The ALJ concluded that the sampling and extrapolation techniques used to determine the amount of the overpayment in this case were flawed. The government's expert con-

---

21. Appendix at sections 1.0 and 1.1

ceded that the samples in these particular cases failed to give the expected precision in the estimates, agreed that the suggested sample size in the Appendix was 320 and that the relative error was far in excess of the target value in this case.[22]

Furthermore, the provider in *Keith O. Irby and Michelle P. Irby, R.Ph.,* July 13, 1994, was successful in arguing that the OIG failed to certify the accuracy of the sampling methodology. In that case, the owner of a medical supply company and his wife were excluded from participating in Medicare and state health care programs as a result of criminal convictions related to fraudulent Medicare claims.

The ALJ concluded that the sampling was invalid because the OIG failed to establish the auditor's expertise in statistics to certify the accuracy of the sampling performed. The OIG offered no evidence as to the statistical validity of the sampling, except to assert that sampling is a valid methodology in determining the amount of overpayments. In addition, the auditor testified during the hearing that the sampling may have been biased in favor of finding overpayments.

## Practical Advice

Theoretically, providers may appeal the validity of a statistical study at any level, including rebuttal and in negotiations with the government agency that performed the audit or that is assessing the overpayment. Contractors may revise overpayment determinations if the provider is able to demonstrate obvious and fundamental errors in their sampling studies; this should generally be a provider's initial approach. Although this approach can be rewarding, usually providers will have to challenge a statistical study's validity in the formal appeal process.

In Medicare Part B cases, the first opportunity to challenge a sampling study's statistical validity will be at the fair hearing level; in Part A cases this will occur at the ALJ hearing. Providers should note that there are many Medicare fair hearing officers who do not believe they have jurisdiction to rule on the validity of sampling studies, although some will rule on this issue. Although their position is incorrect, the issue can be raised for the first time at the ALJ appeal. Additionally, there are a small number of ALJs who do not believe they have jurisdiction to rule on this issue. The ALJ should make that decision on the record so it can be appealed to the MAC.

Health care providers should review all relevant data to determine if other errors in the statistical process exist, such as mathematical errors in computing the aggregate overpayment. In addition, providers should look for *underpayments*—situations where Medicare paid less than the appropriate amounts for legitimate services. These can often be used to offset the overpayment amount using the same extrapolation methods used by the Carrier to compute the overpayment.

The first step in appealing a sampling study is usually to retain an expert statistician who can guide the provider or its counsel through this highly technical area. It is best to retain an expert early so that he or she can assist in the development of the case, including providing guidance as to what documentation should be requested. However, not all overpayment determinations may be large enough to justify the expense of an expert. Some purely legal issues can be raised without an expert, particularly the absence of required documentation. Providers have won appeals at both the fair hearing and ALJ levels without the use of experts, but more often than not, they are necessary.

---

22. *Respi Flow, Inc.,* October 15, 1998; Clinical Lab Work Corp., January 9, 1998

The selection of the expert statistician is a critical choice. Because of the technical and sometimes complex nature of the issues involved, communication skills, both written and verbal, are essential. The expert must be able to discuss very technical subject matter at a level that is understandable to all parties. The use of analogies from everyday life is useful to help the decision maker grasp the concepts thoroughly. Most ALJs and hearing officers are not familiar with these issues so the expert must educate them during the course of the hearing or through the written report or affidavit. If the education process does not happen, the hearing is likely to have a disappointing outcome.

## Conclusion

Although challenging the validity of a sampling study used to assess an overpayment can be a daunting task for the statistics novice, including most providers and their counsel, it is an essential aspect of any appeal of such cases. With regard to overpayment cases, this issue may be the only realistic one available to appeal in those cases in which the provider's arguments on the substantive issues leading to the overpayment are not winners. Winning a challenge to a sampling study can result in significant savings on an overpayment assessment.

CHAPTER 3

# Retrospective Versus Contemporaneous Reviews

## Thomas E. Boyle and Robert B. Ramsey, III

The elimination of health care fraud has become a high priority for the federal government. The number of health care fraud investigations, both civil and criminal, has risen dramatically in recent years. The total amount of fines and assessments associated with these investigations is truly astronomical. In order to avoid costly investigations and fines, health care providers are well advised to implement effective compliance programs that are designed to prevent noncompliance with the host of laws and regulations applicable to the health care industry.

The advantages of effective compliance programs are numerous. One significant advantage is the avoidance of government investigations since compliance programs are inherently designed to prevent noncompliance before it occurs. As noted in the Department of Health and Human Services' Office of Inspector General's (OIG's) *Compliance Program Guidance for Hospitals*, "[t]he adoption and implementation of voluntary compliance programs significantly advance the prevention of fraud, abuse and waste . . . while at the same time furthering the fundamental mission of all hospitals, which is to provide quality care to patients."[1]

The OIG further states it believes an effective compliance program is a "sound investment" for hospitals to make. Today, most providers have adopted a corporate compliance program designed to ensure compliance with the myriad complex laws and regulations impacting the health care industry.

Most compliance programs incorporate the seven key elements universally recommended by the federal government in its numerous pronouncements regarding compliance programs.[2] One of the seven key elements, audits and reviews, is absolutely essential for the success of any compliance program. A careful review or audit of a provider's

---

1.  63 F.R. 8987 (February 23, 1998)

2.  The seven key elements recommended by the OIG of the Department of Health and Human Services effective compliance program are: (i) written code of conduct; (ii) designation of a

programs and activities is critical to determining the organization's level of compliance with the extremely complex set of rules and standards applicable to health care providers.

The importance of internal reviews is emphasized in a number of government pronouncements. For example, the Federal Sentencing Guidelines provide that:

> The organization must have taken reasonable steps to achieve compliance with the standards, by utilizing monitoring and auditing systems reasonably designed to detect criminal conduct by its employees and other agents and by having in place and publicizing a reporting system whereby employees and other agents could report criminal conduct by others within the organization without fear of retribution. [*Federal Sentencing Guidelines*, Comment 3.(k)(5)]

In a similar fashion, the model compliance guidance published by the OIG also emphasized the importance of self- reviews and audits. In its model guidance published for the hospital industry, the OIG stated:

> An ongoing evaluation process is critical to a successful compliance program. The OIG believes that an effective program should incorporate thorough monitoring of its implementation. . . . Although many monitoring techniques are available, one effective tool to promote and ensure compliance is the performance of regular, periodic compliance audits by internal and external auditors.[3]

Similar statements have been made in the OIG's model guidance published for other segments of the health care industry.[4]

While it is quite clear that audits and reviews are absolutely essential to the success of an effective compliance program, questions remain as to the manner of conducting such reviews. One unanswered question relates to the appropriate time period on which the audit should focus. Much debate and discussion have arisen over whether compliance reviews should be limited to current, contemporaneous matters or whether the review should also include a retrospective review of matters from the past for which payment has already been received from a third party payor. This is certainly a critical question that, unfortunately, is without a clear, definitive answer. The answer will depend on the particular facts and circumstances confronting a health care provider. An important factor that should be considered in this analysis is the provider's underlying objective for conducting the review; other important factors include the risk of prosecution for a crime, the likelihood of further review by the government and the relevant statute of limitations.

---

[2 continues] chief compliance officer and other appropriate bodies such as a corporate compliance committee; (iii) effective education and training programs; (iv) hotlines and similar processes; (v) the use of audits, reviews, and other evaluation techniques to monitor compliance; (vi) enforcement of compliance standards through well published disciplinary standards; and (vii) the investigation and remediation of identified systemic problems and policies addressing the nonemployment or retention of sanctioned individuals.

3. 63 F.R. at 8996

4. In its model Guidance published for the long-term care industry, the OIG stated that it "believes that an effective program should incorporate thorough monitoring of its implementation and ongoing evaluation process." See *Fed. Reg.* 14289, 14302 (March 16, 2000).

## The Goals of a Review

A logical starting place for a discussion of the goals of a review is the statements promulgated by the federal government on the subject of compliance. Unfortunately, such statements, while providing some guidance, do not fully answer the question regarding an appropriate time frame for a review. However, general principles applicable to this issue can be gleaned from various government pronouncements.

As quoted above, the federal Sentencing Guidelines indicate that an organization must take steps "reasonably designed" to detect illegal conduct. Note the use of the term "reasonably designed." A provider must, therefore, take whatever steps it believes to be reasonable in order to effectively evaluate compliance. Such reasonable steps must be tailored to the particular facts and circumstances. While in some cases a contemporaneous review may suffice, in other situations the facts and circumstances may dictate a retrospective review.

The OIG provides a greater discussion of this issue in its model compliance guidance for hospitals wherein it states:

> Monitoring techniques may include sampling protocols that permit the compliance officer to identify and review variations from an established baseline. *Significant variations from the baseline should trigger a reasonable inquiry to determine the cause of the deviation.* If the inquiry determines that the deviation occurred for legitimate, explainable reasons the compliance officer, hospital administrator or manager may want to limit any corrective action or take no action. If it is determined that the deviation was caused by improper procedures, misunderstanding of rules, including fraud and systemic problems, the hospital should take prompt steps to correct the problem.[5]

The OIG also notes in a footnote to its model compliance guidance that a provider should take a "snapshot of their operations from a compliance perspective." The OIG then goes on to state that "[t]his snapshot, often used as part of benchmarking analyses, becomes a baseline for the compliance officer . . . to judge the hospital's progress in reducing or eliminating potential areas of vulnerability." Such a baseline snapshot will provide an initial assessment of compliance. If the baseline assessment indicates that the provider is in substantial compliance, the provider can use that assessment to benchmark future compliance. However, what if the initial review indicates a deeply rooted, potentially long-standing problem? In such circumstances, a provider must be prepared to take whatever steps are "reasonably designed" to assure compliance.

While the statements of the government are generally helpful, they do not specifically answer the question of how far back a provider must look when conducting a review. The authors believe that in analyzing this question it is helpful to review the provider's goals and objectives for conducting a particular audit or review.

Audits and reviews are conducted for a variety of reasons. As noted above, some are conducted to provide a baseline from which to measure future performance and to judge the provider's current state of compliance. This is the "snapshot" referred to in the OIG's model guidance. Another objective of many reviews is to investigate specific complaints or suspicions regarding areas identified by the government as potentially problematic. Those specific complaints or suspicions will typically dictate the extent of retroactive review

---

5. 63 F.R. at 8996

required. Still another reason for a review is to comply with the mandates of a corporate integrity agreement (CIA). Obviously, in this latter circumstance, the scope and length of the review will be clearly delineated in the CIA, which is negotiated with the government; the provider must conduct the review accordingly or face significant penalties.

Regardless of the reason for the review, all such reviews are undertaken for the purpose of making some determination regarding the organization's level of compliance. In that regard, the scope of the review must be designed to assess whether, and to what extent, the organization is complying with applicable standards. Thus, an organization must be prepared to conduct a review of sufficient duration to assure itself of the organization's actual compliance with the applicable law or regulation. To do anything less would not be in keeping with the general standard of being "reasonably designed" as mandated in the federal Sentencing Guidelines.

## Contemporaneous Reviews

Some commentators within the compliance industry have advocated limiting reviews and audits to contemporaneous matters. As a result, some providers have limited the scope of a compliance assessment to a contemporaneous review, mistakenly believing that such a limited review will also limit the scope of the potential liability and afford greater flexibility for dealing with the results of the review. Clearly, in certain circumstances, contemporaneous reviews offer a distinct advantage by affording the provider the opportunity to correct a problem before it even becomes an issue or before the issue grows to a significant magnitude. Typically, the contemporaneous review involves matters that either have not yet been billed by the provider or have not yet been paid by the third party payor. Under such circumstances, the matter can be corrected before it might be considered a false or fraudulent claim. In such situations, the contemporaneous review offers obvious distinct advantages. However, in many circumstances, further review is likely to be warranted and, in some cases, absolutely necessary if the provider is to avoid severe consequences.

The authors believe that providers who limit their reviews solely to contemporaneous matters may be, in many cases, exposing their organization to significant legal and financial risks. Without question, contemporaneous reviews are necessary and appropriate to determine an initial baseline view of a particular billing practice or activity. However, in some instances, the contemporaneous review should represent only the beginning of the review process. To the extent that material deviations from expected norms are uncovered during the contemporaneous review, it will often be the case that similar deviations occurred in the past. Ignoring past problems in such situations is not without risk. In order to avoid these risks the provider will need to conduct a thorough review of all relevant time periods.

## Disclosure Obligations

As noted above, the provider that ignores the retroactive implications of a contemporaneous review may potentially be exposing itself to significant risks. One such risk relates to the complex issue regarding the disclosure obligations of providers. Although the law in this area is less than clear, the potential for serious consequences is a distinct possibility for the provider that attempts to knowingly hide past mistakes.

The subject of disclosure obligations has been somewhat controversial. However, the potential for criminal liability for failure to disclose exists. Certain provisions of the Social Security Act have been interpreted to impose a criminal penalty for failure to disclose knowledge of the receipt of overpayments. The Social Security Act provides:

> Whoever—having knowledge of the occurrence of any event affecting (A) his initial or continued right to any such benefit or payment, or (B) the initial or continued right to any such benefit or payment of any other individual in whose behalf he has applied for or is receiving such benefit or payment, conceals or *fails to disclose* [emphasis added] such event with an intent fraudulently to secure such benefit or payment either in a greater amount or quantity than is due or when no such benefit or payment is authorized, . . . shall (i) in the case of such a statement, representation, concealment, failure, or conversion by any person in connection with the furnishing (by that person) of items or services for which payment is or may be made under the program, be guilty of a felony, and upon conviction thereof fined not more than $25,000 or imprisoned for not more than five years or both. [42 USC § 1320a-7b(a)(3)]

This section of Medicare law has been the subject of substantial debate.[6] Government prosecutors have publicly taken the position that the knowing failure to refund Medicare or Medicaid overpayments constitutes a violation of this law. In addition, government enforcers predict increased use of this law to prosecute health care providers who retain funds that are clearly overpayments. Under the government's theory, retention of overpayments constitutes a felony even if the funds were originally obtained through a billing mistake (or even an error by a third party such as the fiscal intermediary) and not by means of illegal or fraudulent conduct. It is the act of retaining such funds, to which the provider knows it was not originally entitled, that forms the basis for the alleged felony. The strength of the government's position is difficult to accurately assess due to several factors. First, there is no case law directly interpreting the government's position under this statute. In addition, little guidance is provided by the scant legislative history of this provision. Also, given the awkward wording of this law, it is subject to several conflicting interpretations. Without case law interpreting it, it is impossible to know with certainty the actual scope of the law. In addition, this provision of the law is sometimes difficult to apply in practice. In some circumstances it is very difficult to determine whether the provider was wrongfully paid. Thus, health care providers are left to ponder the risks of nondisclosure. However, given the severe penalties possible under this law, providers must exercise a significant amount of caution when dealing with potential overpayment situations.

The relevance of this law to our discussion of contemporaneous versus retroactive review is quite obvious. Contemporaneous reviews offer the advantage of pinpointing current problems. In many situations, however, it is quite clear that an inference can be drawn from the contemporaneous review that similar problems occurred in the past. Ignoring the potential existence of past problems, as inferred from a contemporaneous review, may constitute a violation of the previously quoted provision of the Social Security Act. From a government prosecutor's perspective, the information gleaned from the contemporaneous review may constitute "knowledge" of the occurrence of an event affecting the provider's

---

6. It goes beyond the scope of this discussion to detail all aspects of the controversy surrounding this provision of Medicare law. However, certain constitutional law issues have been raised regarding this provision and there has been some debate as to whether it applies only to individuals and not to corporate entities such as hospitals and other health care providers.

right to continued payment. If so, the failure to conduct a retroactive review of the matter and to return any overpayments may constitute a federal felony.

Accordingly, the authors submit that providers must be extremely cautious when implementing an action plan based solely on a contemporaneous review. If the results of the contemporaneous review can be reasonably extrapolated to prior time periods, certain conclusions regarding the propriety of payments during the prior time period can be made. In such a case further review may be warranted. Thus, the analysis of the question of how far back to review begins to take on some clarity. Retrospective reviews offer the organization a mechanism for addressing a situation that, if ignored, could escalate into an extremely serious problem. The question remains, however, as to exactly how far back to conduct the retroactive review.

## Avoidance of *Qui Tam* Actions

An organization that fails to conduct a review covering a sufficient time period may be exposing itself to an increased risk of a *qui tam* (or "whistle-blower") lawsuit under the federal False Claims Act. The number of *qui tam* actions has risen dramatically in recent years and is likely to continue to rise in the future, as more health care workers are educated regarding the law. A well designed compliance program usually includes training on a wide range of topics, including the right of private individuals to bring an action against a provider in the name of the government under this law. This type of employee education may result in the continued rise in the number of *qui tam* actions, especially in circumstances in which an organization has inadequately addressed an issue identified by its compliance efforts.

As discussed above, a contemporaneous review provides a good baseline for measuring compliance since it provides a snapshot of the current state of a provider's operations. However, not only can these reviews identify issues that need to be addressed both immediately and on a "go forward" basis, but they may also uncover past issues that were never addressed. In certain circumstances, it will be obvious that an issue identified during a contemporaneous review was also a problem in the past. Some providers may focus solely on correcting the problem so it will not continue in the future. However, ignoring past problems, particularly those involving overpayments that the provider was not entitled to, can result in substantial risk to the provider. When an issue has been clearly identified and there are many employees within the organization who may know of the problem, the likelihood of a whistle-blower suit increases significantly if the provider does not take steps to address the issue. A provider organization should assume that more than a handful of individuals within the organization are aware of the problem. Under these circumstances, it is likely that a *qui tam* action will be filed, especially if the employee perceives reluctance on the part of the provider to do the right thing. Such a threat can be adequately disposed of, however, by conducting a retrospective review and following up with disclosure to the appropriate government agency if necessary.

One of the risks associated with this approach is the increased exposure to *qui tam* actions under the federal False Claims Act because of employees or contractors who know or subsequently learn of the results of the contemporaneous review. In some circumstances, if it is obvious that a problem uncovered during a contemporaneous review has been ongoing for quite some time, self-disclosure for the entire relevant period reduces the possibility of a whistle-blower lawsuit. A federal district court in Illinois recently gave support to this position. In *United States ex rel. Cherry v. Rush Presbyterian/St. Luke's Medical Center,*[7] the Northern District Court of Illinois held that a voluntary disclosure by a provider has the legal effect of being a public disclosure under the False Claims Act. Accordingly, the whistle-blower was barred from proceeding with the *qui tam* action. The False Claims Act includes a number of jurisdictional bars, including a section that bars court jurisdiction regarding allegations that have been publicly disclosed.[8] The District Court in *United States ex rel. Cherry* held that self-disclosure by a Medicare provider to government officials constitutes such a public disclosure, thereby raising the jurisdictional bar for the subsequent *qui tam* action.

Whenever a provider is aware of but chooses to ignore the existence of current or past problems, it is likely that some employees either know or suspect a problem exists. Any one of these employees represents a possible whistle-blower who might bring the problem to the government's attention. By expanding the contemporaneous review to include a retrospective review, the provider can gain control over the situation and can be in a position to get the best possible treatment for its mistake through the self-disclosure process.

## Likelihood of Further Review by the Government

Another relevant factor to consider in determining the appropriate time period for review is the time period that is most likely deemed relevant by the federal government. This is especially true in situations where a provider is making a self-disclosure based on a contemporaneous review. The Centers for Medicare and Medicaid Services (CMS, formerly the Health Care Financing Administration or HCFA) has issued special instructions to its fiscal intermediaries regarding unsolicited or voluntary refund checks received from providers. Under certain circumstances, fiscal intermediaries are instructed to perform a detailed analysis of the situation giving rise to the refund check, including a determination as to whether further review is appropriate. When making a decision regarding further review, fiscal intermediaries are instructed to "consider whether the refund accurately reflects the full disclosure of the debt."[9] Thus, in situations where a provider conducts a less than complete review of the past history of a problem and attempts to resolve the matter by self-disclosure to the intermediary, the likelihood of further review appears to be substantial. Not only will the provider end up with liability for its undisclosed past behavior, it is likely to have significantly undermined its credibility in such a case.

## Statute of Limitations

The statute of limitations applicable to the False Claims Act is also relevant to the discussion of how far back a provider may need to go when conducting a retrospective review. A provider that is attempting to analyze the pervasiveness and ramifications of a particular

7. *United States ex rel. Cherry v. Rush-Presbyterian/St. Luke's Medical Center,* 2001 WL 40807 (N. Dist. Ill. January 16, 2001)

8. 31 U.S.C. § 3730(e)(4)

9. HCFA Program Memorandum, HCFA Pub. 60 AB, Transmittal No. AB-00-41 (May 1, 2000)

issue will certainly want to view the matter from the same viewpoint as the government, and it is quite likely that the government will review the matter for the entire time period open under the statute. However, determining the exact length of the statute of limitations is sometimes difficult because it is complicated by the statute's discovery rules. It is further complicated by the government's aggressive interpretation of the statute and its discovery rules. Nonetheless, the statute of limitations does provide at least some framework for limiting exposure and, therefore, provides a potential time parameter for a retrospective review.

The statute of limitations under the False Claims Act provides that a cause of action may not be brought after a certain period of time, specifically whichever is later: either six years after the violation is committed or

> Three years after the date when facts material to the right of action are known or reasonably should have been known by the official of the United States charged with responsibility to act in the circumstances, but in no event more than ten years after the violation is committed. [1 U.S.C. § 3731]

The language of the statute of limitations has been the subject of some dispute and several key issues have yet to be completely and adequately resolved. For example, there has been a considerable amount of case law developing around the question of who is the government official charged with responsibility to act. Some courts have limited this question to the appropriate Department of Justice official. Other courts have taken a broader view and have included other agents of the government whose duty it is to investigate health care fraud. Another question impacting the statute of limitations is what constitutes the "facts material to the cause of action." Once again, federal court decisions have been inconsistent regarding this issue and no clear answer can be found. Thus, providers are typically faced with a statute of limitations under the False Claims Act that potentially varies from a minimum of six years to a maximum of 10 years.

In reality, the statute of limitations provides only minimal guidance for conducting a retrospective review. To the extent an issue has likely occurred for some time, there is a fairly strong likelihood the government can assert a claim for at least six years. On the other hand, it is possible that the government might have an argument in certain circumstances to extend the statute of limitations for up to 10 years. Whether a provider should conduct the retrospective review for at least six years or longer will depend on the particular facts involved.

## Conclusion

A key component of all corporate compliance programs are audits and reviews. A critical question, however, is how far back a provider must go in conducting an audit or review. Many factors will impact this decision and the answer to the question will vary from situation to situation. Contemporaneous reviews offer the advantage of providing a baseline "snapshot" assessment of a provider's compliance with the law. However, in many circumstances the results of a contemporaneous review will lead to the conclusion that further review of past practices should be conducted. Failure to conduct a retrospective review in such circumstances will expose the provider to potential legal risk.

# CHAPTER 4

# The Attorney-Client Privilege in the Context of Health Care Compliance Investigations

## Jan Murray, Dorothy Regas Richards and David Rowan

T his chapter provides an overview of the attorney-client privilege and certain other legal doctrines that apply to disclosure of communications that are made during the course of a corporate compliance investigation. The elements of the privilege are examined as well as the limits of the privilege and the manner in which it may be lost or waived. The chapter also describes considerations that relate to the privilege and affect key decisions about the structuring of a corporate compliance investigation, and includes a list of tasks that should be undertaken to maximize the protections afforded by the privilege.

This chapter is not intended to serve as an exhaustive treatment of a complex legal doctrine, but rather to offer a useful outline to legal practitioners and compliance officers regarding the privilege and its application to an internal investigation. The focus of the chapter is on application of the doctrine by the federal courts because many significant health care investigations have been based on the federal False Claims Act, although differences in state law are noted because state authorities have an important role in enforcement as well.

## Attorney-Client Privilege

The attorney-client privilege is a common law concept. Federal Rule of Evidence 501 applies this common law privilege as interpreted by the federal courts to federal actions. Evidence Rule 501 also provides that where an element of a claim or defense is based on state law, state law will also govern the privilege of a witness. In some states, the attorney-client privilege is defined in state statute, and in others the common law privilege is applied in the courts. See, for example, *Simon v. G.D. Searle & Co.*, 816 F.2d 397 (8th Cir. Minn. 1987), involving a products liability diversity action for the court's analysis of the application of Minnesota law defining the scope of the privilege.

The attorney-client privilege is generally defined as confidential communication between a client and his or her lawyer for the purpose of obtaining legal advice or securing legal services and not for the purpose of committing a crime or tort. The specific elements of the privilege were defined in *Rhone-Poulenc Rorer Inc. v. Home Indemnity Co.*, 32 F.3d 851, 862 (3d Cir. 1994). According to the Court:

> Communications that may be protected from disclosure during discovery because of the attorney-client privilege possess the following characteristics: (1) the asserted holder of the privilege is or sought to become a client; (2) the person to whom the communication was made (a) is a member of the bar of a court, or his or her subordinate, and (b) in connection with this communication is acting as a lawyer; (3) the communication relates to a fact of which the attorney was informed (a) by his client (b) without the presence of strangers (c) for the purpose of securing primarily either (i) an opinion of law or (ii) legal services or (iii) assistance in some legal proceeding, and (d) not for the purpose of committing a crime or tort; and (4) the privilege has been (a) claimed and (b) not waived by the client.

## Identity of the Client

Application of these elements to business entities that provide health care services is sometimes complex. The attorney-client privilege involves a communication between an attorney and a client; however, in the context of a large corporation, the identity of the client may be a difficult task. *Upjohn Co. v. United States*, 449 U.S. 383 (1981), is a leading case that rejected the application of the so-called "control group" theory and applied a more functional definition of "client" within the context of the privilege.

*Upjohn* involved an investigation conducted under the aegis of the company's General Counsel in response to certain findings by company auditors regarding illegal payments to foreign officials. To investigate the findings, the General Counsel sent a letter and questionnaire to managers in the field who were most likely to have knowledge of the payments. Concluding that these employees were the "client" for the purposes of the privilege, the Court reversed the Court of Appeals order enforcing an administrative subpoena issued by the Internal Revenue Service seeking the managers' responses.

In rejecting the lower court's conclusion that these employees were not sufficiently high-ranking to fall within the company's "control group," the Court noted that the privilege necessarily embraces information from the client to the attorney that is necessary for the attorney to formulate advice. In the *Upjohn* case, these lower ranking employees were crucial sources of information and, in fact, had been directly involved with the matter under investigation. If these employees were not the "client" for the purpose of applying the privilege, the privilege would be meaningless. However, the *Upjohn* court formulated three limitations: first, the information must be communicated for the express purpose of securing legal advice; second, the communication must relate to the specific corporate duties of the employee; and third, it must be treated as confidential within the corporation itself.

Another distinction that is relevant to *public* health care providers is the rule that applies to government clients and counsel. Many states limit the application of the rule when the client is a government entity or official. The *Revised Uniform Rule of Evidence* 502(d)(6) limits the privilege of the governmental entity; this approach has influenced many states. Also see In re *Lindsey*, 158 F.3d 1263 (D.C. Cir. 1998), for a discussion of the application of the privilege in a matter involving communications between federal government attorneys and government officials arising from a grand jury investigation of former President Bill Clinton.

The privilege may apply not only to lower ranking employees but also to former employees and company consultants. If the matter in dispute relates to actions taken by these individuals on behalf of the company, and if the information communicated by them to the attorney is necessary for the attorney to formulate his or her advice, the communication should be privileged as well.

Many states do not follow *Upjohn*. Some adhere to a control group theory, and some state courts or legislatures have crafted quite different approaches (e.g., the "subject matter" approach analyzed by the Florida court in *Southern Bell Tel & Tel Co. v. Deason*, 632 So.2d 1377 [1994]). Some state courts have very broadly defined the word "client" to include all employees of the represented entity. In an interesting case that arose in a health care setting, the Oregon Supreme Court concluded that any employee is a representative of the client for purposes of defining what communications are privileged. The decision involved remarks by the Chair of the Anesthesiology Department to other faculty members; the court ruled that his remarks did not constitute a disclosure to outside parties (*State ex rel. Oregon Health Sciences Univ. v. Haas*, 942 P.2d 261 [1997]).

In some investigations, it may become apparent that certain employees or agents were acting outside the bounds of their employment and had taken action to further their own interest rather than act in the company's interest. In this situation, it is important for the counsel to warn the employee that he or she represents the corporation and not the employee and, as such, will not be acting in the interest of the employee. The American Bar Association *Model Rules of Professional Conduct* obligates the attorney to provide a corporate "Miranda" warning to the employee involved (see Rule 1.13[d]). The rule provides:

> In dealing with an organization's directors, officers, employees, members, shareholders or other constituents, a lawyer shall explain the identity of the client when it is apparent that the organization's interests are adverse to those of the constituents with whom the lawyer is dealing.

Also see In re *Bevill, Bresler & Schulman Asset Management Corp.*, 805 F.2d 120 (3d Cir. 1986), where the court rejected a claim of privilege by a corporate officer because the privilege could only be asserted by the corporation that had waived it.

## Nature of Communications

The attorney-client privilege applies to communications made by a client; the privilege does not apply to the underlying facts of the communication. The court defined this distinction in *Rhone-Poulenc Rorer, Inc. v. Home Indemnity Company*:

> Facts are discoverable, the legal conclusions regarding those facts are not. A litigant cannot shield from discovery the knowledge it possessed by claiming it communicated it to a lawyer. [32 F.3d 851, 864].

The purpose of the privilege is to ensure that clients are able to communicate freely to their attorneys without fear of disclosure. The federal courts have, however, defined the privilege to extend to the attorney's communication to the client. The 9th Circuit articulated this viewpoint in *United States v. Bauer*:

> At the outset, it is important to recognize that the attorney-client privilege is a two-way street: 'The attorney-client privilege protects confidential disclosures made by a client to an attorney in order to obtain legal advice, . . . as well as an attorney's advice in response to such disclosures.' [*United States v. Chen*, 99 F.3d 1495, 1501 (9th Cir. 1996) (132 F.3d 504, 507)]

This position does not mean that all communications made by counsel to a client are privileged; only legal advice is included in the privilege. Other statements reflecting facts may not be covered. According to the court in *United States v. United Shoe Mach. Corp.*, 89 F. Supp. 357 (D. Mass. 1950):

> Where a communication [from counsel] neither invited nor expressed any legal opinion whatsoever, but involved the mere soliciting or giving of business advice, it is not privileged. [*United States v. Vehicular Parking*, D.C Del, 52 F. Supp. 751 (89 F. Supp. 357, 359)]

However, some state courts have issued widely varying opinions about whether the protected communication includes the attorney's advice to the client. Although most courts provide some protection to the advice given the client, a minority provides complete protection to that advice.

Another significant limitation of the definition of protected communication relates to documents that are prepared by the client prior to the moment in time when the attorney began preparations to give advice. Documents that were created prior to an investigation are not typically included in the privilege. See *United States Postal Serv. v. Phelps Dodge Ref. Corp.*, 852 F. Supp. 156 (E.D.N.Y. 1994), where the court declined to extend the privilege to scientific reports prepared by consultants prior to the time counsel was consulted.

The attorney-client privilege only applies to those communications—oral or written—that are actually made in confidence. Therefore, it is extremely important to ensure that all communications are made in private settings and that a system is in place (as discussed later) to secure the confidential treatment of documents that are privileged. Similarly, communications made in the presence of third parties are not privileged because they have not been made confidentially—unless these third parties are acting as agents to counsel. Therefore, the privilege can be lost by careless communications made in public places where the parties would not reasonably be expecting privacy. See *United States v. Bay State Ambulance & Hosp. Rental Service, Inc.*, 874 F.2d 20 (1st Cir. 1989).

## The Definition of Counsel

The identity of the lawyer may also be contentious in the context of a health care investigation. Most large health care entities employ in-house counsel. Communications to in-house counsel enjoy the same degree of protection as do those made to outside counsel; however, staff counsel occasionally perform other executive duties in addition to their duties as counsel. In that case, the courts will determine whether counsel was acting as an attorney or primarily as a business person (see, e.g., *United States Postal Serv. v. Phelps Dodge Ref. Corp.*, 852 F. Supp. 156 [E.D.N.Y. 1994]).

Typically, an "attorney" for the purpose of the privilege is a lawyer licensed to practice law in the jurisdiction where the advice is rendered. However, some courts recognize application of the privilege to lawyers who are not licensed in that jurisdiction but are licensed to practice in some other jurisdiction, as the court did in *Paper Converting Machine Co. v. FMC Corp.*, 215 F. Supp. 249 (E.D. Wis. 1963). This case involved a patent lawyer's advice provided to a client in Ohio; the lawyer was not licensed in Ohio, but the court concluded he still had the "status of an attorney" (215 F. Supp. 249).

The privilege also applies to employees or agents of the attorney who are performing at the direction of the attorney to investigate a matter in which the attorney has been retained to provide advice. These people may include not only paralegals and secretaries but also auditors or other professionals retained by the attorney specifically to develop facts for the purpose of advising a client. See, for example, *United States Postal Serv. v. Phelps Dodge Ref. Corp.*, supra.

# Waiver of the Privilege

The attorney-client privilege may be waived directly by the client, inadvertently through careless disclosure of the information or by operation of law.

## Direct Waiver

Because the privilege belongs to the *client*, only the client may waive the privilege and permit disclosure of otherwise confidential documents or communications. A third party may not waive the privilege unless, of course, counsel is waiving the privilege with the client's consent. For example, courts have held that an unauthorized leak of confidential information by an employee does not constitute a waiver of the privilege by the corporate client. See *Smith v. Armour Pharmaceutical Co.*, 838 F. Supp. 1573 (S.D. Fla. 1993).

## Inadvertent Waiver

Inadvertent waiver of the privilege may occur if appropriate steps are not taken to maintain the confidentiality of the information gathered during the investigation. In fact, when an inadvertent waiver does occur, the courts will examine the steps taken by client and counsel to protect the information from inadvertent disclosure.

*Gray v. Bicknell*, 86 F.3d 1472 (8th Cir. 1996), involved the mistaken disclosure of privileged information: namely, two letters written by counsel to his client analyzing certain aspects of the dispute. Neither party disputed the privileged nature of the communications. The opinion describes three approaches followed by courts in ruling on the effect of an inadvertent disclosure. The first approach concludes that if a disclosure is inadvertent, it does not waive the privilege because waiver must be intended. The second approach, at the opposite end of the spectrum, holds that any disclosure, whether or not inadvertent, serves to waive the privilege. The third and more intermediate approach examines several factors, including what steps were taken to protect the communication from disclosure, when the mistake was discovered, and whether it serves the interests of fairness to rule that a waiver has occurred. See also *Pavlik v. Cargill, Inc.*, 9 F.3d 710 (8th Cir. 1993).

Disclosure of confidential information to others in the corporate family, however, does not automatically constitute a waiver of the privilege by the client.

To maintain confidentiality, the investigative team should control the flow of information and limit communications to specifically identified people. Outside consultants or experts who are brought in to participate on the team should be retained directly by counsel. In addition, outside consultants and experts should submit all reports—properly marked as confidential and subject to attorney-client privilege—to the attorney designated to lead the investigation.

## Waiver by Operation of Law

In certain cases, the privilege may be waived by operation of law, either by evidentiary rules or implementing regulations.

**The crime-fraud exception.**   The most common example of this type of waiver involves the crime-fraud exception. This exception is an evidentiary rule that permits discovery of communications between a lawyer and the client if they are in furtherance of a future or on-going crime or fraud, since such communications are considered outside of the scope of the attorney-client privilege. See *United States v. United Shoe Mach. Corp.*, 89 F. Supp. 357 (D. Mass. 1950), in which the Court defined the privilege as applicable when a client communicates with an attorney for the purpose of securing legal assistance "and not for the purpose of committing a crime or tort."

Thus, the client's intent when communicating with an attorney is key in determining whether privilege exists. The exception applies even if the lawyer is not aware that the client's purpose in seeking the advice is to perpetrate a crime (*United States v. Chen*, 99 F.3d1495 [9th Cir. 1996]). However, the exception does not apply to instances of past conduct. Thus, the timing of any improper communications could be critical in determining which documents may be protected. See In re *Grand Jury Proceedings*, 604 F.2d 798 (3d Cir. 1979), in which the court held that the client could protect certain documents if it showed that they were prepared after the alleged crime took place and before the client consulted with counsel. According to the court, if the alleged crime took place before communications with counsel, the privilege would apply. Thus, the crime-fraud exception applies if the party seeking disclosure can satisfy two requirements: (1) establish a *prima facie* case that the client committed or intended to commit the fraud, and (2) prove that communications with the lawyer were intended to further the fraud or were reasonably related to it. See In re *National Mortg. Equity Corp. Mortg. Pool Certificates Litigation*, 116 F.R.D. 297 (C.D. Cal. 1987).

The crime-fraud exception was first recognized more than a century ago, although it was originally applied in cases in which the party was actually being tried for the crime. See *Alexander v. United States*, 138 U.S. 353 (1891). More recently, the exception resulted in the waiver of the privilege in *United States v. Anderson* (No. 98-20030-01) (D. Kan. March 9, 1999), which involved the indictment of two health care lawyers for allegedly assisting in a scheme to violate the federal anti-kickback statute. Although the judge acquitted the lawyers after trial, the hospital executives and physicians were convicted.

**Exception for reliance on advice of counsel.** The attorney-client privilege is also treated as waived in situations where a client's defense to an action rests on its reliance on the advice of counsel. Courts generally treat this situation as a direct waiver or as an outcome required in the interest of fairness. See *Accord Johnson v. Rauland-Borg Corp.*, 961 F. Supp. 208 (N.D. Ill. 1997), involving waiver of the privilege by asserting that the defendant had acted reasonably in retaining counsel to investigate a matter. Therefore, whenever a client asserts that he or she embarked on a course of action "on the advice of counsel," the court will likely rule that the privilege is waived.

**Regulatory waivers.** In addition to evidentiary rules, the federal government has made significant efforts to limit the applicability of the privilege in the context of a corporate compliance investigation. See, for example, *The Office of Inspector General's Corporate Compliance Guidance for Hospitals*, 63 Fed. Reg. 8987, February 23, 1998. The government's self-disclosure protocol requires that the provider give the government full access to all audit work papers and other documents without assertion of privileges or limitations. The Office of Inspector General of the Department of Health and Human Services (OIG), however, does state that it will not usually request production of written communication that falls under the attorney-client privilege; but if it determines that it needs such documents, the OIG will discuss with the provider's counsel ways to obtain the information (*Provider Self-Disclosure Protocol*, 63 Fed. Reg. 58399, October 30, 1998). This "let's discuss it approach" does not apply in cases involving search warrants or subpoenas *duces tecum* issued by the regulatory authority or the court; in these cases, the matter must be referred to court.

While disclosure of all relevant facts is required to participate in the voluntary disclosure program, such disclosure may have the practical effect of waiving the privilege. It is very difficult to make a case for "selective" waiver of the privilege. See, for example, *Westinghouse Elec. Corp. v. Republic of Philippines*, 951 F.2d 1414 (3d Cir. 1991), involving efforts by the corporation to assert the attorney-client privilege after voluntarily disclosing the same documents to the Securities Exchange Commission. In *United States v. Massachusetts Inst. of Tech.*, 129 F.3d 681 (1st Cir. 1997), the university was held to have waived the privilege *and the attorney work product protection* by disclosing the documents to a U.S. Department of Defense auditing agency.

## Privilege Considerations in a Corporate Compliance Investigation

The attorney-client privilege is the doctrine most commonly applied to protect and preserve the confidentiality of communications during an internal compliance investigation. However, the attorney-client relationship alone is not enough to establish a presumption that communications and documents are privileged. See In re *Woolworth Corp. Secs. Class Action Litig.*, 166 F.R.D. 311 (S.D.N.Y. 1996). The other elements of the privilege must be present in order to be enforced.

Therefore, clients and their counsel must take affirmative steps to maintain the confidentiality of documents and assert the privilege to protect communications and/or documents at any point should disclosure be sought. To determine whether the privilege has been maintained, courts will examine whether the confidentiality of communications has been protected on a consistent basis throughout the duration of the investigation.

Compliance officers should first ascertain who should conduct the investigation. In general, if a nonlawyer conducts the review, the material will not be protected unless another privilege happens to apply to certain documents (e.g., in health care, the physician-patient privilege or peer review privilege may apply). In determining whether counsel should direct the investigation, compliance officers need to assess at the outset the possibility of criminal or civil sanctions or penalties that may result from the investigation. Routine activities such as periodic monitoring of operations to assess compliance generally are not conducted under the direction of counsel unless the compliance officer has reason to suspect the existence of facts that will result in the corporation having to affirmatively disclose inappropriate conduct and take remedial action. Finally, if the matter that will be investigated is a matter in which the compliance officer has had previous involvement (e.g., gave advice or was otherwise aware of the activity), then he or she should turn the matter over to counsel to avoid any questions regarding conflict of interest.

If an attorney conducts the investigation, the organization should decide whether to use in-house legal staff or outside counsel. Use of outside counsel may be optimal for investigation of any matter that is likely to have serious consequences so that the applicability of the privilege is clear. If in-house legal staff is selected to direct the investigation, the attorney involved needs to clearly document that he or she is serving as counsel and not in another capacity (e.g., as compliance officer). Similarly, if the corporate compliance officer is also a lawyer and is selected to participate in the investigation in his or her capacity as an attorney, there needs to be correspondence in the file that clearly defines the role that he or she performs for that specific investigation. However, unless the corporate compliance officer's job description includes rendering of legal advice and, consequently, the job qualifications include a license to practice law, he or she may not be viewed by a court as counsel to the organization. Moreover, if the corporate compliance officer has a law degree but does not have a license to practice law in that jurisdiction, many courts will not extend the privilege to the compliance officer because they will not extend the privilege to communications with an unlicensed attorney.

In addition, consider taking the following steps to establish and preserve the attorney-client privilege during an internal investigation:

1. When initially contacting counsel, clarify that the purpose is to seek counsel and then do so confidentially (e.g., do not invite an auditor or consultant to the initial meetings).
2. Define the investigative strategy between counsel and the compliance officer:
   a. Counsel may wish to seek written authorization from the highest corporate officer to initiate an investigation, for purposes of establishing the intention to protect privilege and the scope of the investigation. This authorization should also indicate to whom (i.e., which employees or officers of the client) the results of an investigation should be reported.
   b. If counsel is directing the investigation, counsel should prepare correspondence authorizing the members of the investigative team to conduct the internal review on behalf of counsel. The correspondence should advise team members to mark all documents produced in conjunction with the review as "confidential and subject to attorney-client privilege" and to address all communications to counsel.
   c. The individuals to be interviewed and documents to be produced need to be identified, as well as who will conduct the interview and who will be present; again, counsel should be present during any interviews to preserve the privilege.
   d. All documents subject to the privilege or other immunity should be marked. It is recommended that counsel maintain a log of privileged documents and keep them filed separately in counsel's office.
   e. Other precautions should be taken as necessary to ensure controlled access to and release of documents and other information, including electronic transmissions of data and communications.
   f. All individuals who become involved in the investigation should be cautioned to maintain the confidentiality of the review.
   g. The organization should be alert to situations in which an employee may have interests contrary to those of the corporation, or who may otherwise require separate counsel. The organization should always clearly communicate to employees (1) who it is that counsel represents and (2) the client's compliance policy, which is to act in accordance with local, state and federal statutes and to take remedial actions as may be necessary depending on the outcome of the review.
3. As necessary, counsel should directly engage the services of outside consultants or experts and require all reports and communications to be issued solely to counsel and to be clearly marked as confidential and subject to the privilege.

## Related Legal Doctrines for Protection From Disclosure

In addition to the attorney-client privilege, there are several other doctrines that may be applied, either individually or in conjunction with the attorney-client privilege, to protect the confidentiality of information related to an internal compliance investigation. Of these, the most often asserted are: (1) the work product doctrine, (2) the self-evaluative privilege and (3) the privilege against self-incrimination.

### The Work Product Doctrine

The work product doctrine offers protection of certain documents from disclosure during the course of discovery. The U.S. Supreme Court originally fashioned the doctrine in *Hickman v. Taylor*, 329 U.S. 495 (1947). In that case, the Court held that the work product of a lawyer had qualified immunity from discovery if that work product was prepared in anticipation of litigation. The doctrine is now codified in federal law in Rule 26(b)(3) of the Federal Rules of Civil Procedure and Rule 16(b)(2) of the Federal Rules of Criminal Procedure.

The work product doctrine differs from the attorney-client privilege in that it protects only documents from discovery (as distinguished from verbal communications), including interviews, memos, correspondence, notes and briefs, which evidence "mental impressions, conclusions, opinions or legal theories of an attorney or other representative of a party concerning litigation" (FRCP Rule 26[b][3]).

The most significant limitation in the application of the doctrine is that the documents to be protected from discovery must have been prepared in anticipation of litigation. This does not mean that a claim actually must have been filed for the doctrine to apply, but there must be more than a remote possibility of a claim in the future. Thus, the doctrine's scope covers documents prepared in anticipation of a grand jury investigation (see In re *Grand Jury Investigation*, 599 F.2d 1224 (3d Cir. 1979)) or in anticipation of a disclosure to the government.

The doctrine encompasses not only documents prepared by counsel but also documents prepared, compiled, or analyzed by nonlawyers and agents of an attorney. See, for example, In re *Dayco Corp. Derivative Sec. Litigation*, 102 F.R.D. 468 (S.D. Ohio 1984), holding that a diary compiled by a corporate employee at the direction of counsel was protected from discovery. Analyses or reports that were prepared before an attorney was involved in the investigation, however, generally are excluded from protection under this doctrine. Materials prepared during the ordinary course of business are generally not covered by the work product doctrine, unless lawyers compile them as part of trial strategy (see below).

Courts often distinguish "fact" work product from "opinion" work product; the latter reflects the attorney's mental impressions about a case or trial strategy. In most cases, courts are reluctant to compel production of "opinion" work product and, instead, prefer to look to the specific circumstances of each case to determine the scope of the privilege. For example, during a deposition about the existence of certain documents, an attorney for a car manufacturer refused to answer, claiming that to testify as to the existence of certain documents in her voluminous files would reflect her judgment, as an attorney, on the importance of certain documents to be used in her client's defense. Although the trial court ruled that testimony regarding the existence of documents was not work product, the Eighth Circuit reversed that decision, stating that "requiring in-house counsel to testify that she is aware that documents exist concerning a certain issue is tantamount to requiring her to reveal her legal theories and opinions concerning that issue." *Shelton v. American Motors Corp.*, 805 F.2d 1323 (8th Cir. 1986). In contrast, see In re *Grand Jury Subpoenas*, 959 F.2d 1158 (2d Cir. 1992), holding that a request for five years of telephone records that were compiled by a client's attorney were discoverable, since the volume was such that the attorney's thoughts or litigation strategy would not be exposed by their production.

As with the attorney-client privilege, the attorney seeking the work product doctrine must take affirmative steps beyond merely asserting the privilege. For example, Federal Rule of Civil Procedure 26(b)(5) requires that, in asserting the doctrine, "the party shall make the claim expressly and shall describe the nature of the documents, communications, or things not produced or disclosed in a manner that, without revealing information itself privileged or protected, will enable other parties to assess the applicability of the privilege or protection." The requesting party then has the burden to show there is a need for the material and that it would impose a substantial hardship on the party to obtain similar material.

In the context of a compliance investigation, the attorney should mark all applicable notes and memoranda as "attorney-work product prepared in anticipation of litigation" to identify specific documents subject to the privilege. As with the attorney-client privilege, the protections afforded by the doctrine may be waived by the "crime-fraud exception." Unlike the attorney-client privilege, disclosure of the documents to an unrelated third party does not automatically waive the privilege. However, disclosure of the documents to an adversarial party will most likely constitute waiver of the privilege for all materials on the same subject matter that were disclosed. Thus, in the case of negotiations with the federal government, production of documents to further settlement discussions is generally considered a waiver of the protections afforded by the doctrine.

## The Self-Evaluative Privilege

The self-evaluative privilege affords clients protection from disclosure of subjective evidence created during the course of an internal investigation and prepared by the parties responsible for conducting the investigation. Unlike the attorney-client privilege or work product doctrine, the material that may be protected under this privilege does not have to have been created by or for counsel; nor is it necessary to have counsel involved in the process.

The self-evaluative privilege was originally fashioned by the courts for purposes of encouraging full internal investigations. See *Webb v. Westinghouse Electric Corp.*, 81 F.R.D. 431 (E.D. Pa. 1978). According to the Webb court, "If subjective materials constituting 'self-critical analysis' are subject to disclosure during discovery, this disclosure would tend to have a 'chilling effect' on an employer's voluntary compliance with equal employment opportunity laws."

In the case of environmental investigations, the privilege has been codified in many states and at the federal level. For example, the federal Environmental Protection Agency promulgated a Policy for Self-Policing that became effective in January 1996. The policy encourages companies to conduct internal investigations and implement corrective actions in exchange for certain enforcement incentives. See "Incentives for Self-Policing: Discovery, Disclosure, Correction, and Prevention of Violations," 60 Fed. Reg. 66706 (December 22, 1995).

In the case of internal health care investigations, many states protect the results of medical peer review proceedings from discovery (see e.g., Ohio Revised Code § 2305.35). Recently, however, accreditation and regulatory bodies have taken steps to dilute the umbrella protections provided through the peer review process. For example, in January 2001, the federal Centers for Medicare and Medicaid Services, formerly the Health Care Financing Administration, announced that it was considering the issuance of draft regulations to require the disclosure of certain documents and information that otherwise may be protected under these peer review statutes ("HCFA Considering Changes in PRO Policy to Clarify Medical Disclosure Instructions," *BNA Healthcare Daily Report* [January 4, 2001]).

Further, new patient safety standards promulgated by the Joint Commission on Accreditation of Healthcare Organizations (JCAHO) became effective July 2001, which require hospitals to inform patients (and, when appropriate, their families) whenever results of care differ significantly from anticipated outcomes ("JCAHO New Tell-All Standards Require that Patients Know About Below-Par Care," *Modern Healthcare* January 1, 2001]).

Because it is generally applied on a case-by-case basis by the courts, the application of the privilege may be very limited depending on the jurisdiction. Thus, other than environmental audits or similar internal investigations for which confidentiality is protected by statute or rule, the results of internal investigations that are not conducted under the direction of counsel are generally subject to disclosure and discovery by adversarial parties.

## The Privilege Against Self-Incrimination

The right against self-incrimination is a personal one; it does not apply to, and may not be asserted by, a corporation or other business entity. Therefore, while it may be available to an executive accused of criminal wrongdoing, it is not available to the corporation or other entity employing that person (*Hale v. Henkel*, 201 U.S. 43 [1906]).

PART

# Voluntary Compliance Monitoring and Auditing

# Financial Relationships With Physicians: Auditing and Monitoring Anti-Kickback Statute and Stark Law Compliance

## Katherine Lauer

The federal government has shown increasing interest in recent years in investigating and prosecuting illegal financial arrangements between hospitals and referral sources. The government arsenal now includes not only criminal penalties under the anti-kickback statute, but also civil administrative penalties under the federal self-referral law (the Stark Law) and the Civil Money Penalties Law (CMPL). In addition to these traditional anti-fraud weapons, the government and private whistle-blowers have begun to invoke the federal False Claims Act in connection with improper referral relationships. Several courts have held that claims "infected" by improper referral relationships can be considered "false," subjecting the provider to treble damages and statutory penalties under the False Claims Act's oftentimes draconian damages provisions.[1]

An effective compliance program can be a provider's best defense against potential scrutiny and investigation. But even the most well conceived set of policies is doomed to failure in the absence of an effective process for auditing and monitoring compliance. Given the complexities of the anti-kickback statute safe harbors and the exceptions to the Stark Law, standard auditing processes focused on statistical sampling, trending and benchmarking have limited application. Instead, a provider must develop tools that will allow it to review its relationships with referral sources systematically, yet efficiently, in a way that focuses resources on identified areas of risk.

This chapter gives a brief overview of the relevant laws. It also addresses some of the primary risk areas that have been identified by the Office of Inspector General of the Department of Health and Human Services (OIG) through its model compliance guidance and in corporate integrity agreements (CIAs). Finally, it discusses various issues that should be considered in developing a program to audit and monitor compliance with laws governing physician relationships.

---

1. See, e.g., *United States ex rel. Thompson v. Columbia/HCA Healthcare Corp*, 20F Supp. 2d 1017 (95.0 Tex 1998); *United States ex rel. Pogue v. American Healthcorp, Inc.*, 914 F Supp. 1507 (M.D. Tenn. 1996).

## The Statutory Framework Surrounding Hospital Financial Relationships With Physicians

### Federal Anti-Kickback Statute

The federal anti-kickback statute, 42 U.S.C. § 1320a-7b(b), is a criminal statute that prohibits transactions that are intended to induce referrals or business paid for by Medicare, Medicaid and almost every other health care program funded by the federal government. The anti-kickback statute prohibits knowingly and willfully soliciting, receiving, offering or paying any "remuneration" in return for or to induce: (1) the referral of an individual for the furnishing of any item or service that may be paid for under a federal health care program; and (2) the purchasing, leasing, ordering, arranging for or recommending of any item or service that may be paid for under a federal health care program.[2]

The OIG has promulgated certain "safe harbors" which, if fully complied with, will ensure that the participants in the arrangement are not prosecuted criminally or civilly under the anti-kickback statute.[3] The OIG has stated that it may exercise its prosecutorial discretion not to pursue a case if the participants appear to have acted in a genuine, good faith attempt to comply with the terms of a safe harbor.[4] Importantly, arrangements that fall outside a safe harbor are not necessarily illegal; the safe harbors merely describe arrangements that are safe from prosecution. Transactions that do not meet the safe harbor criteria are examined on an individual basis to determine compliance with the anti-kickback statute.[5] The OIG has also issued "fraud alerts" and "advisory opinions" that clarify the government's position with respect to certain activities and the anti-kickback statute.

### Physician Self-Referral Prohibition: The Stark Law

The Stark Law generally prohibits a physician from making referrals of Medicare and Medicaid patients for the furnishing of certain "designated health services" to any entity with which the physician has a financial relationship, unless a statutory or regulatory exception applies to the arrangement. The "designated health services" include, among other things, hospital inpatient and outpatient services, diagnostic radiology services and clinical laboratory services. The Stark Law also prohibits entities from presenting any claim for payment with respect to designated health services rendered pursuant to a tainted referral.[6] Unlike the anti-kickback statute, where compliance with a safe harbor is not mandatory but protects arrangements from prosecution, entities cannot present claims for

2. Conviction of an anti-kickback statute violation results in a fine of $25,000 or imprisonment for not more than five years, or both. In addition to these criminal penalties, the Department of Health and Human Services (HHS) has authority to impose civil money penalties of (i) up to $50,000 and (ii) three times the amount of remuneration in question, for each violation of the statute. Violations of the anti-kickback statute can also result in exclusion from participation in federal health care programs, including Medicare and Medicaid.

3. See Medicare and State Health Care Programs: Fraud and Abuse; OIG anti-kickback Provision, 56 Fed. Reg. 35,952, 35, 954 (July 29, 1991).

4. Id., note 8

5. Id.

6. 42 U.S.C. § 1395nn(a)(1)

payment with respect to designated health services unless an arrangement fits within one of the Stark Law exceptions. The Stark Law is not an intent-based statute.

A "financial relationship" is defined broadly, and includes any direct or indirect relationship between a physician (or a physician's immediate family member) and an entity in which the physician or family member has (1) an ownership or investment interest or (2) a compensation arrangement.[7] A compensation arrangement means any arrangement involving any direct or indirect payment, discount, forgiveness of debt, or other benefit made directly or indirectly, overtly or covertly in cash or in-kind between a physician (or a member of the physician's immediate family) and an entity.[8]

## OIG Guidance on the Components of a Successful Physician Relationship Compliance Plan: Identification of Issues for Review

### *OIG Compliance Program Guidance for Hospitals:* Identification of Risk Areas

In February 1998, the OIG issued its *Compliance Program Guidance for Hospitals* (the Hospital CPG).[9] Although focused primarily on reimbursement and the claims process, the Hospital CPG also addresses financial relationships between hospitals and physicians and other referral sources. The Hospital CPG requires, for example, the development of written standards of conduct, policies and procedures that address hospital relationships with physicians, and other health care professionals. It also identifies certain types of financial arrangements the OIG perceives as posing substantial compliance risk.[10]

**Identification of risk areas.** The OIG identified the following specific risk areas implicating physician financial relationships:

▶ *Hospital incentives that violate the anti-kickback statute or other similar federal or state statutes or regulations.* The OIG specifically pointed to "excessive payment for medical directorships, free or below market rents or fees for administrative services, interest free loans and excessive payment for intangible assets in physician practice acquisitions" as examples of arrangements that may violate the anti-kickback statute.[11]

▶ *Joint ventures.* The OIG indicated that it is particularly concerned about business arrangements established between those in a position to refer business and those providing items and/or services that may be billed to federal programs.[12]

---

7. 42 U.S.C. § 1395nn(a)(2)

8. 42 U.S.C. § 1395nn(h)(1)

9. *Office of Inspector General's Compliance Program Guidance for Hospitals* (February 1998). The Hospital CPG, as well as the OIG's other compliance program guidances can be found at *http://www/hhs/gov/progorg/oig/modcomp/index.htm.*

10. *Id.* at 7

11. *Id.* at 17 and n. 23

12. *Id.* at 18 and n. 24

▶ *Financial arrangements between hospitals and hospital-based physicians.* The OIG expressed its concern with so-called "reverse kickbacks," arrangements where hospital-based physicians perform services for less than fair market value or pay over market for services provided by the hospital in exchange for which the hospital makes referrals to the hospital-based physician.[13]

▶ *Stark physician self-referral law.* The OIG expressed its concern that physician financial relationships may violate the self-referral provisions of the Stark Law, but did not provide additional commentary.[14]

**Development of policies and procedures.**  To address the above risk areas, the OIG prescribes that a hospital compliance program establish policies and procedures requiring that:

▶ All of the hospital's contracts and arrangements with referral sources comply with all applicable statutes and regulations.

▶ The hospital does not submit or cause to be submitted to the federal health care programs claims for patients who were referred to the hospital pursuant to contracts and financial arrangements that were designed to induce such referrals in violation of the anti-kickback statute, Stark physician self-referral law, or similar federal or state statutes or regulations.

▶ The hospital does not enter into financial arrangements with hospital-based physicians that are designed to provide inappropriate remuneration to the hospital in return for the physician's ability to provide services to federal health care program beneficiaries at the hospital.[15]

**Auditing and monitoring compliance.**  An important component of the OIG's compliance guidance involves auditing and monitoring compliance with established policies and procedures. The OIG considers such activities critical to a successful compliance program. It suggests regular, periodic compliance audits by internal or external auditors who have expertise in federal and state health care statutes and regulations. These audits must be designed to address hospital compliance with the laws governing kickback arrangements and the Stark physician self-referral prohibition. The OIG suggests that audit procedures also address compliance with the specific rules that have been the focus of the OIG's Special Fraud Alerts.

The OIG also suggests that the audit process include on-site visits, interviews with personnel, questionnaires (to solicit information from employees regarding the hospital's activities), reviews of financial records and other supporting documents, and trend analysis or longitudinal studies (to ascertain deviations in specific areas over a given period).[16]

Other than broadly suggesting "sampling protocols" and the identification and review of variations from established "baselines," the Hospital CPG provides very little guidance

---

13.  *Id.* at 18 and n. 25

14.  *Id.* at 19

15.  *Id.* at 28. The OIG suggests that facilities' in-house counsel or compliance officer should collect, *inter alia*, OIG regulations, special fraud alerts, advisory opinions regarding compliance with the anti-kickback statute, the Civil Money Penalties Law (CMPL) and Stark. It further suggests that policies should reflect and reference the applicable OIG anti-kickback Safe Harbor Regulations. *Id.*

16.  *Id.* at 42-45

on how an organization should audit and monitor physician relationship compliance. Indeed, the vast majority of OIG guidance regarding auditing and monitoring tools applies to billing, coding and other areas where statistical sampling and "benchmarking" can effectively be used to identify areas of potential noncompliance.

In the physician relationship area, however, these statistical tools may have little, if any, application. The information necessary to determine whether a facility's physician relationships comply with the anti-kickback statute and Stark Law is often maintained in different departments, frequently maintained in hard copy rather than electronically, and, particularly where there has been substantial turnover in senior administration, often lacking in uniformity.

Providers are not, however, without government guidance in this area. Recent CIAs that have been entered into in conjunction with settlements with the federal government contain detailed criteria for the auditing and monitoring of physician relationship compliance. These CIAs reveal not only the risk areas defined as significant by the OIG, but also specific auditing techniques the OIG considers acceptable to identify and correct noncompliance.[17]

## Corporate Integrity Agreements: The "Outlier" Approach

Recent CIA workplans use an "outlier" approach to physician relationship auditing. Certain types of relationships are identified as posing the greatest risk of noncompliance with applicable law. Various criteria are then developed for each relationship type, the presence of which serves as an indication of potential noncompliance. Relationships that have these criteria are identified as "outlier" relationships, which are then subject to further review. Legal personnel review the outliers, conduct additional factual investigation, determine whether the relationship is compliant and recommend corrective action, if necessary. Relationships determined to be noncompliant are included in periodic reports, which track not only the problem but the status of corrective action as well.

Recent CIAs have identified the following physician relationships as having the greatest risk of noncompliance:

▶ Loans and other physician accounts receivable that are past due
▶ Leases of buildings where physicians have offices
▶ Personal services agreements (medical directorships and consultancies) and other payments to physicians

The following are examples of the types of criteria the OIG uses to identify outliers:[18]

▶ **Overdue loans and other past due accounts.** Outlier is defined as a receivable that meets both of the following criteria: (a) is over 120 days delinquent and (b) has not been referred to outside counsel within 30 days of becoming 120 days delinquent.

---

17. Using existing CIAs as a guide in developing an organization's voluntary compliance program has additional benefits in the event the organization finds itself liable for civil or criminal violations. Not only does the risk of exclusion decrease, the risk that the OIG will require the organization to undertake the significant burdens and expenses associated with a mandatory CIA decreases as well. This is because the OIG has, under some circumstances, allowed organization to maintain their existing compliance programs rather than requiring the organization sign a CIA. The more the existing plan addresses the OIG's concerns, the more likely the OIG will accept that plan.

18. The approach discussed herein was used in the HCA (formerly Columbia/HCA) CIA, which became effective December 2000. This CIA contains a detailed Physician Arrangements Workplan, and is available in its entirety from the OIG pursuant to the Freedom of Information Act.

▶ Medical office building leases. Outlier is defined as a lease that has one or more of the following characteristics: (1) lease is not in writing, (2) rent payable is not consistent with fair market value (fair market value to be determined without taking into account the volume or value of any referrals or other business generated between the parties), (3) lease terms are not commercially reasonable and (4) rental payments are not current and appropriate collection activities are not being pursued.

▶ Personal service agreements and/or payments to physicians. Outlier is defined as a relationship that has one or more of the following characteristics:
  - Payments made to a physician: (a) without a written contract, (b) inconsistent with the contract services rendered as required by the contract
  - Personal services agreements (excluding hospital-based physicians) that provide for: (a) compensation of more than the specified hourly rate (e.g., $150/hr) without a fair market value verification by an independent third party, or (b) more than 40 hours work per month by the physician without a fair market value verification by an independent third party (unless the greater number of hours is required by applicable statutes or regulations)

▶ Multiple medical directorships at the same facility with the same apparent function where the physicians are not demonstrated co-directors

▶ Leases of physician-owned property or equipment without a fair market value verification from an independent third party

▶ Physician recruitment arrangements that: (a) do not meet the Stark II[19] physician recruitment exception, (b) involve the recruitment of a physician with an active practice located within 25 miles of the facility, (c) have repayment/forgiveness terms of over four years, (d) involve payments for overhead greater than the marginal overhead increase when a physician is recruited to join a group practice or (e) are not supported by a certificate of community need

It is important to keep in mind that, under this approach, a relationship designated as an "outlier" is not necessarily noncompliant. Rather, the criteria represent "red flags" that may indicate potentially problematic relationships. Consequently, the next step in the process is a detailed review of the "outlier" relationships by legal personnel, including an examination of all relevant facts through document review and interviews with facility personnel. The facility should review the contract terms and the parties' adherence to them, the facility's need for the services described in the contract and those actually provided, evidence of payments to the physician, physician referral patterns, evidence of work actually performed (such as contemporaneous time records), indications of fair market value, and the commercial reasonableness of the arrangement.

The results of this review are then memorialized in a database, including documentation of: (1) the findings and conclusions for each relationship reviewed; (2) any corrective action necessary to bring the relationship into compliance; (3) a corrective action plan, if necessary; (4) preparation of a disposition form for each outlier reviewed and (5) preparation of periodic summary reports on the status of corrective actions.

---

19. The expansion of the Stark Law to the other designated health services is often referred to as "Stark II."

# Developing the Audit Protocol

The OIG guidance helps providers identify general risk areas, as well as specific issues to be considered in connection with various types of physician relationships. But identifying the "right" questions to ask is only the first step in developing an audit protocol. There are many details to consider in putting together a compliance methodology for monitoring and auditing physician relationships. The following is a discussion of several options a provider may want to consider.

## Defining the Universe

One of the first things an organization may want to do is define the universe of relationships subject to review. If the organization has one or a small number of facilities, the task of auditing physician relationships may not be terribly daunting. Indeed, if the universe of arrangements is small, it may be feasible to examine each arrangement individually. In multihospital systems, on the other hand, there may be hundreds, or even thousands, of physician arrangements potentially subject to review. In those circumstances, it is likely the organization will want to develop a methodology that will allow it to effectively audit a sample of representative relationships in a cost-effective manner.

**Types of relationships subject to audit.** The organization should consider including each of the following types of physician arrangements in its audit program:

▶ Personal services agreements, consulting agreements, medical directorship agreements and other arrangements in which payments are made to physicians
▶ Leases of medical office building space to physicians
▶ Loans and other physician accounts owed to the facility
▶ Recruiting agreements
▶ Joint ventures between hospitals and physicians
▶ Employment agreements
▶ Acquisition or leases of physician-owned property by the facility
▶ Lavish gifts and entertainment and other benefits provided to physicians

**Determining sources of available data.** The scope of review will depend, to some extent, on existing data sources. Thus, the organization should determine what data sources are readily available and contain information relevant to compliance issues. For example, there may exist internal compliance reviews, surveys or routine audits that collect some of the information necessary to evaluate compliance with physician relationship policies. There may also exist centralized electronic accounting databases that may contain information regarding payments owed for rents, loans and other physician accounts, or electronic accounts payable data showing amounts paid to physicians and other similar compilations. Some sophisticated organizations may even have developed a comprehensive database of physician contracts that list relevant contract terms and track performance to ensure the parties comply with the contract.

Obviously, the more electronic data that is available, the easier it will be to survey a wide range of relationships. Searches can be developed using the existing databases, the results of which can then be forwarded to compliance or legal personnel for additional review. For example, if the organization tracks physician accounts receivable electronically through its general ledger or some other database, it could periodically flag all accounts that are more than 120 days past due without appropriate collection activities.

Even if there is significant electronic data, it will still be necessary to perform some review of source documentation at the facility level. The organization will need to determine how its various facilities maintain relevant documents and electronic source data, and will then have to develop a protocol identifying which sources of information should be reviewed for audit. Again, the more data that is stored electronically, the more likely searches can be developed that would allow a wide range of relationships to be reviewed.

The following suggests some of the types of documents and other files that typically contain the information that should be examined during an audit of physician relationships:

▶ Physician contract files
▶ Deal documents produced in connection with acquisitions
▶ Memoranda, correspondence, letter agreements and other documentation reflecting the negotiation, modification and performance of the arrangement, including any "side agreements" or oral modifications
▶ Attorney opinion letters
▶ Rent rolls or other documents indicating payments of rental obligations
▶ General ledger and other accounts receivable data indicating payments on loans, promissory notes or other accounts
▶ Demand letters and other documents reflecting efforts to collect rents, loans and other accounts receivable from physicians, including documents reflecting the settlement or compromise of any amount owed by physicians or other referral sources to the hospital as a result of legal action
▶ Accounts payable files, W-2s, 1099s, check registers, cancelled checks, invoices, time records and other documents supporting payments made to physicians in connection with medical directorships and other personal services agreements
▶ Appraisals, market surveys, independent valuations, published industry salary data and other information relied upon to support fair market value determinations
▶ Referral/admissions data

**Defining the population subject to review.** Once the types of relationships to be reviewed have been identified, and after the determination of what data are available and how difficult this information is to retrieve, the organization will be ready to determine the scope of review. Unless the total population is so small that regular review of all arrangements is practicable, the organization will want to define a subset of the population subject to review.

One way to narrow the scope of review is to review only a portion of the population during any given review cycle. In a multifacility system, audits may be conducted at only a portion of the facilities each year. For example, an organization may choose to audit one-third of its hospitals each year so that each hospital is examined once every three years. Another option is to use existing data sources to identify facilities that are having more compliance problems, and to concentrate audit resources—at least initially—in those facilities. For example, the organization might want to focus its attention on facilities that have excessive delinquent physician accounts, have a large number of medical directors, or those that have been identified as potentially problematic through hotline complaints or other compliance channels.

Even within each facility subject to audit, the organization may want to concentrate on only a portion of the physician population. Because both the anti-kickback statute and the Stark Law are concerned with improper remuneration in connection with referrals of government program patients, one way to limit the scope of review is to look only at physicians who make such referrals to the facility. Not all facilities keep track of referrals, but billing data should be available that show the "admitting" and/or "attending" physician.

Another way to limit the potential scope of review, yet capture those relationships most likely to be problematic, is to establish a materiality threshold. For example, the facility may want to look only at physicians who generated a certain minimum level of gross charges, or the top 10 or 20 admitting physicians.

## Selection of the Audit Team

The next step in developing an audit protocol is the selection of the audit team. Many organizations—particularly large hospital systems—may already have an existing internal audit staff. Others may have significant in-house legal resources. Smaller systems may rely on outside auditors and lawyers. The first issue is whether to use lawyers, nonlawyer accountants and auditors, or some combination of the two. Consideration should be given to the availability of personnel, the cost of outside resources and the size of the population to be audited. Existing electronic databases and other compilations of existing data will also play into the decision of who should conduct the audit. For example, if the organization has a comprehensive physician contracts database that includes information on basic contract terms and information about contract performance, much fieldwork can likely be avoided. Similarly, if the organization has comprehensive electronic records on physician accounts receivable or on performance of rental obligations, audits can be performed on a broader scope with use of fewer resources.

The composition of the audit team will determine, to a large extent, the protocol to be used in data review.  If the audits are conducted largely by in-house or outside lawyers who have expertise in evaluating the legality of financial arrangements with referral sources, it may not be necessary to provide detailed checklists or other tools. Rather, the lawyers can likely be relied upon to evaluate the relationships according to the applicable statutes and regulations, and to identify compliance issues without extensive checklists or worksheets. Similarly, if the organization requires legal review at the time each physician arrangement commences, then the focus can shift away from basic contract terms to the performance of the arrangement. Under such circumstances, an abbreviated audit process may be appropriate.

On the other hand, if the audits are performed primarily by nonlegal personnel, who may be less familiar with the intricacies of safe harbors and Stark exceptions, then the organization will likely need to develop standard worksheets, checklists or electronic audit programs that specify for the audit team the information that is to be collected. If an outlier approach were employed, for example, nonlegal personnel might use detailed criteria and/or checklists to identify the outliers. Once information has been gathered in the field regarding the outlier arrangements, it can then be forwarded on for legal review. This review determines whether a particular relationship complies with applicable statutory and regulatory requirements and, if it does not, appropriate corrective action is recommended.

## Developing Detailed Audit Criteria

**Identify areas of compliance risk.**  As it develops its audit tools, the organization will want to identify specific areas of compliance risk. The organization should start with the anti- kickback statute safe harbors, the Stark Law exceptions and the specific types of arrangements identified in the OIG's Fraud Alerts, the Hospital CPG and recent CIAs. The criteria discussed above provide comprehensive, although not exhaustive, guidance on the government's "hot buttons" in this area.

The organization should then perform an assessment of its own physician arrangement compliance controls and processes to identify other areas of risk specific to the organization. These additional identified risk areas should then be incorporated into the audit program. For example, the organization may have strong policies regarding up-front legal review of its contracts to ensure all medical directorship agreements are compliant on their face, but may have weak accounting controls that result in payments made without written contracts in place, payments made after written contracts have expired or payments made without required backup or time support.

Alternatively, an organization may do a good job of ensuring that all of its medical office building leases are consistent with fair market value and are otherwise compliant, yet it may have poorly coordinated collection functions allowing significant delinquencies to develop. Similarly, the organization might enter into recruiting agreements that fully comply with all regulatory requirements, yet it does not have an infrastructure in place that vigorously pursues collection of income guarantee repayments.

One control that may be particularly weak involves monitoring the submission of claims to ensure compliance with the Stark Law's prohibition on the submission of bills for services that were provided pursuant to prohibited referrals. The Stark Law, by its terms, prohibits not only the financial relationship; it provides that entities shall not submit claims for—and that the government shall not pay for—designated health services referred by physicians with prohibited financial relationships. Technically, in order to comply with this prohibition, an entity must not only monitor its physician relationships to ensure that its physician arrangements fit within one of the Stark Law's exceptions, it must also monitor its billing activities to ensure it does not submit claims that are not compliant with the Stark provisions.

The OIG also suggests in the Hospital CPG that providers refrain from submitting bills for services provided as a result of illegal kickbacks.[20] Providers face additional risk under the False Claims Act, which has been interpreted by several courts that have ruled that claims infected by kickbacks can be "false."[21] In the past few years, a number of FCA actions, particularly those filed by *qui tam* Relators, have tested the traditional limits of liability under the Act, in a wide variety of contexts. Several FCA cases have been filed based at least in part on alleged violations of the anti-kickback statute and Stark Law. In many of these cases, the Relators have crossed the initial threshold of stating a legal basis for asserting that such a violation renders subsequently filed claims false. Some of the cases, such as *United States ex rel. Pogue v. American Healthcorp, Inc.*, rely on the contention that the provider implicitly certifies compliance with federal health care fraud and abuse statutes by virtue of its participation in the federal Medicare program, rendering claims submitted on referrals tainted by illegal kickbacks false.[22] Other cases, like *United States ex rel. Thompson v. Columbia/HCA Healthcare Corp.*, include both the implicit certification theory and additional allegations that the explicit certification contained in HCFA Cost Reports constitutes an actionable false claim if there is an underlying violation of the anti-kickback statute or Stark Law.[23] To date, relatively few reported decisions deal with these issues, most of which involve motions to dismiss rather than consideration of liability and damages.

---

20. OIG Hospital CPG at 28

21. See *United States ex rel. Thompson v. Columbia/HCA Healthcare Corporation*, 20 F. Suppl. 2d 1017 (S.D. Tex. 1998); *U.S. ex rel. Pogue v. American Healthcorp, Inc.*, 914 F. Suppl. 1507 (M.D. Tenn. 1996).

22. 914 F. Supp. 1507 (M.D. Tenn. 1996)

23. 20 F. Supp. 2d 1017 (S.D. Tex. 1998)

**Develop an audit checklist.** Once the organization has gained a complete understanding of its physician relationship processes and controls, and has identified risk areas specific to the organization, it can begin to create a meaningful audit checklist. Criteria should be developed for each type of relationship, with particular attention given to areas where the organization's performance has been weak in the past. At this point, counsel should be consulted to ensure the checklist accurately reflects all the requirements of current law and regulation. The lawyers and auditors should work together to develop a protocol that is comprehensive, yet manageable, so it may be applied by individuals with no legal training.

## Sample Checklist

While each organization should develop its own checklist, the following is an example of a checklist that includes not only the specific issues identified by the OIG, but various other requirements of the anti-kickback statute safe harbors, the Stark II statute, and relevant OIG Advisory Opinions and Fraud Alerts. This checklist is comprehensive enough to not only identify outliers but to collect much of the basic factual data that would be needed by legal personnel reviewing whether a relationship complies with applicable laws and regulations. The following characteristics are indicative of noncompliant physician relationships.

1. **Personal services agreements**
   ▶ Payment not set out in advance or appears to take into account volume or value of referrals or business
   ▶ Referrals required
   ▶ No written contract to support payments; written contract expired, but payments still being made and/or services still being provided; or payments differ from amounts specified in contract
   ▶ Multiple medical directorships with the same apparent function where the physicians are not demonstrated co-directors
   ▶ Physician holds multiple personal service agreements for administrative services
   ▶ Medical directorship or other personal services agreements for questionable services
   ▶ No time records on file to support payments; no record of services provided in exchange for payments and/or suggestion that physician was told he did not have to provide any services in exchange for payments
   ▶ Payments appear excessive for services provided (e.g., in excess of fair market value, or exceeding a predefined amount—such as $150/hr—without a fair market value certification)

2. **Employment agreements**
   ▶ Amount of payment appears to be based on referrals or takes into account value or volume of inpatient or outpatient services, or hospital ancillary services
   ▶ Payments appear excessive for services provided
   ▶ Payments differ from compensation reflected in written agreement

3. **Leases** (both space and equipment)
   ▶ No written agreement, or written agreement expired, but payments still being made at original lease amount
   ▶ Lease payments vary according to volume or value of referrals, or volume of referrals appears to have been considered in lease payment amount
   ▶ Rent appears to be below fair market value

▶ Excessive lease concessions such as build-out allowance, long-term free rent, free parking, reduced common area maintenance, or other benefits that bring rental rate to below fair market value
▶ Leased space used for something other than legitimate business purpose
▶ Aggregate rent is not set in advance; per "unit" or per "service" rent payments
▶ Sublease of space back to hospital for greater than lease amount to physician
▶ Lease by hospital of space in physician-owned building for what appears to be greater than fair market value, or for space that is unused, underused or not required by hospital for a legitimate business purpose
▶ Rent past due without appropriate collection activities (e.g., referral to outside counsel within 120 days of delinquency)
▶ Past due rent uncollected, written off or transformed into an unsecured promissory note
▶ "Side letter" or oral agreements that vary with the terms of the written lease
▶ Periodic lease arrangement where the lease does not specify intervals when the space or equipment is being leased, and the per interval charge
▶ Physician occupying space without a written lease and without payment of rent

**4. Recruiting agreements**
▶ No written agreement
▶ Contract provides for subsidies (direct or indirect) to an existing practice
▶ Excessive number of recruits into an existing practice
▶ Payments for overhead greater than marginal overhead increase when physician recruited into existing practice
▶ Recruitment of physician with an active practice located within 25 miles of the facility
▶ Repayment/forgiveness terms exceed four years
▶ No certificate of community need
▶ No documentation of reimbursed expenses (e.g., receipts)
▶ Contract payment terms appear to be determined in a manner that takes into account volume of referrals
▶ Contract includes a requirement to refer or to recommend referrals to hospital
▶ Income guarantees exceeded and excess not collected; write-off of loans not legitimately forgiven under contract terms
▶ Amount of guaranteed income not consistent with fair market value; total recruitment package appears excessive

**5. Physician loans**
▶ Loan for personal rather than business purpose
▶ Loan does not appear to bear interest at competitive rate (i.e., above the prime rate)
▶ No written agreement, or written agreement does not reflect terms of the actual agreement
▶ Loan past due over 120 days without referral to outside counsel for collection
▶ Loan past due with no collection efforts
▶ Loan that may be "forgiven" if physician refers patients to the hospital
▶ Suggestion that physician was told that loan does not have to be repaid
▶ Loan balance written off without supporting legal opinion
▶ Loan unsecured
▶ Loan to group not personally guaranteed by physicians

**6. Acquisitions**
▶ Appears that fair market value may not have been paid/received
▶ No independent appraisal done in connection with purchase/sale

▶ No legal opinion done prior to purchase/sale
▶ Valuation considers revenue to hospital from purchaser/seller referral stream
▶ Suggestions of a quid pro quo of referrals in exchange for acquisition and/or significant change in physician referral pattern following transaction
▶ Transaction cannot be justified as a good business deal unless referral stream is taken into account
▶ Sale to physician of hospital-owned property where physician is allowed to "pay" with a promissory note, and note subsequently became delinquent or is forgiven
▶ Indications in proposals, letters of intent, hospital meeting minutes, hospital budgets, correspondence with physician or anywhere else that acquisition was targeted with the intent of capturing the referrals of the selling physicians

### 7. Joint ventures with physicians

▶ Investors are chosen because they are in a position to make referrals[24]
▶ Physicians anticipated to make a large number of referrals are offered greater investment opportunity than those anticipated to make fewer referrals
▶ Physician investors actively encouraged to make referrals to the joint venture
▶ Physician investors encouraged/required to divest their ownership interest if they fail to sustain an "acceptable" level of referrals
▶ Joint venture tracks sources of referrals and distributes information to physician investors
▶ Physician investors required to divest ownership interest if they cease to practice in the service area (e.g., if they move, become disabled or retire)
▶ Investment interests nontransferable
▶ Value of hospital contribution not reflected in ownership percentage (i.e., amount of physician investment disproportionately small)
▶ Hospital bears more than proportionate share of expenses
▶ Hospital distribution is less than proportionate share of revenues
▶ Return on physician investment disproportionately large when compared to other similar investments and/or risk of the particular arrangement
▶ Value of physician interest/distributions varies based on the volume or value of physician referrals
▶ Physician investors invest only a nominal amount (e.g., $500 to $1,500)
▶ Physician investors permitted to "borrow" the amount of the "investment" from the hospital, and pay it back through deductions from profit distributions, thus eliminating any cash contribution to the joint venture
▶ Physician investment paid by hospital

### 8. Entertainment/Gifts/Benefits for referral sources[25]

▶ Physician trips sponsored and paid for, at least in part, by facility
▶ Physician "galas," extravagant parties, expensive dinners, golf outings, major sporting events tickets
▶ "Prizes" and "contests" in connection with performing required tasks such as completing medical records in a timely manner

---

24. The OIG identified a number of what it called "questionable features" of "suspect joint ventures" in its 1994 *Special Fraud Alert* addressing Joint Venture Relationships, which was published in the Federal Register December 19, 1994. The checklist incorporates these features.

25. Many of these physician incentives are identified by the OIG in its 1994 *Special Fraud Alert* addressing suspect Hospital Incentives to Referring Physicians, which was published in the Federal Register December 19, 1994.

▶ Free office equipment, including nondedicated computers

▶ Hospital payment for personal assistants, nurses, therapists, office staff, etc.

▶ Hospital payment for travel to continuing medical education seminars

▶ Free meals or supplies to physician office staff

▶ Hospital provides free transportation to physician's patients

▶ Hospital gives physician discounts on lab services or pharmacy supplies

▶ Gifts, payments or other benefits to physicians who meet referral "goals"

▶ Condominiums provided to physicians for personal use

▶ Country club memberships

▶ Automobile subsidies

▶ Hospital provides marketing and advertising or billing services to physician practice for below fair market value

▶ Lavish holiday gifts

▶ Coverage through hospital's group health insurance plan or malpractice plan at inappropriately low cost to physician

CHAPTER

# Developing a Voluntary Disclosure and Refund

## Alan Peterson and Catherine Sreckovich

I n addition to designation of a Chief Compliance Officer and implementation of a strong compliance team, another important feature of an effective compliance program is the creation of policies and procedures that address matters such as billing adjustments, practice changes, disclosures and possibly voluntary refunds. A health care provider with a compliance program should plan for and practice internal and external communications that relate to billing adjustments, voluntary disclosures and voluntary refunds. Communications regarding billing adjustments and refunds should be conducted early on with the company's internal management, and possibly with the Board of Directors and the revenue-providing funding sources. Such adjustments and refunds should be thoroughly explained, and the provider should be willing to consider how similar billing problems can be avoided in the future.

It can be quite helpful to disclose plans about future and forward-looking reviews and compliance plans, particularly to internal staff. For example, the Chief Executive Officer can appreciate a compliance team's plan for resolving disclosure issues. However, a health care provider will harm its credibility if it makes exaggerated assertions of forward plans, especially if those plans are not successfully or timely executed.

The importance of having reasonable plans in place for making a voluntary disclosure and possible refund cannot be stressed enough. Having such a plan in place can significantly influence the dollar amount of a disclosure and refund settlement, as well as help to preserve a health care provider's credibility and reputation. Moreover, organizations should develop a customized plan for voluntary disclosure that is appropriate to each local situation and organization. This is important because the area of voluntary disclosures and refunds for health care providers is broad and relatively new. While the United States Department of Health and Human Services' Office of Inspector General (OIG) issued an official protocol for voluntary disclosure in 1998, these guidelines are new and relatively untested.[1]

---

1. As is regulatory practice in the United States, the government guidelines are "one size fits all" and are not necessarily the best or most appropriate approach.

The federal government's guidelines for voluntary self-disclosure value prompt and quality information. However, a health care provider cannot obtain quality information to support its voluntary refund without an adequate plan and timely efforts to obtain that information. Information that is not of reasonable quality can be detrimental to the organization. If the information initially offered is of poor quality, a company may have to repeat an overpayment review. In addition, the release of poor quality information regarding a voluntary disclosure can be damaging to a health care provider's reputation and can be a public relations disaster. Timely communication is also important in a situation involving a voluntary disclosure and refund.

## Communicating About Regulatory Interpretations

The compliance program should implement practical interpretations of regulations, organizational rules and guidelines for compliance. Often such interpretations, organizational rules and guidelines should be provided to relevant parties, such as carriers or fiscal intermediaries, insurers, and government entities such as the Department of Health and Human Services' Centers for Medicare and Medicaid Services (CMM, formerly the Health Care Financing Administration) or Office of Inspector General. Such interpretations, organizational rules and guidelines also should be made available to the auditors from these organizations as they conduct their field review work. If a provider communicates its interpretation of regulations to relevant parties in advance of a voluntary disclosure or potential refund, that provider may be able to reduce the size of a possible refund by shortening the time frame of a potential overpayment for which it is responsible. Compliance teams far too often overlook such communications, which require courage. Such communications can help clear up an area of health care regulatory confusion and inconsistency as well as possibly create an environment of what is sometimes referred to as "equitable estoppel"— both of which lead to more efficient operations.

## Identifying High-Risk Areas to Review

A health care provider considering a voluntary refund should first acknowledge that a goal of 100 percent accuracy—whether in billing, coding, cost reports or other areas—is not possible. Rather, the goal should be reasonable and responsible accuracy under the circumstances.[2] After coming to terms with this fact, a health care organization should establish priorities. One step in developing a plan for a voluntary refund is to identify the high-risk areas on which the organization needs to focus; for example, in the billing area, the organization is most likely to be vulnerable to billing errors and potential overpayments. The organization should determine its risk areas that require analysis, such as the frequency of complicated office visits (possible "upcoding," for example). Identifying such areas is an important step in the self-monitoring process.

---

2. Most health care regulatory organizations recognize this realism. See also the Department of Defense's "Ten Key Elements."

## Working Closely With Counsel

Many organizations make the mistake of not involving legal counsel in communications with the federal government during disclosure and refund situations. Leaving attorneys out of the disclosure process can compromise a health care provider's attorney-client privilege.

Counsel can be helpful in most communications that occur during settlement proceedings or future disclosure situations. For example, there are occasions when a health care provider makes a preliminary disclosure regarding a questionable billing or other practice, and the subsequent investigation finds no problem with the practice. In this situation, legal counsel can often guide the organization out of the disclosure process and attempt to try to prevent legal action against the organization.

## Planning and Conducting the Self-Disclosure and Refund Review

Health care voluntary self-disclosure and refund analyses involving the United States government should include a sufficient amount of information related to the possibly erroneous, improper or illegal practice, including:

▶ Identification of the source of the practice at issue
▶ The organization's departments that are associated with the practice in question
▶ The government agency, carrier or fiscal intermediary that has been or may have been affected by the practice in question
▶ Any potential fraud issues raised by the practice and relevant documentation of those issues
▶ The time period during which the practice appears to have occurred
▶ Corporate officials and employees who knew of, encouraged or participated in any improper or illegal practice, if any

The provider will also need to determine an estimate of the dollar impact of the practice on the federal health care programs involved.

In addition to providing sufficient information regarding the erroneous or potentially fraudulent practice, a health care provider should develop sufficient information regarding its response to the erroneous, improper or potentially illegal practice. For example, a health care provider should have a description of how the practice in question was identified. It should also develop

▶ A carefully worded description of the organization's activities related to investigating and documenting any improper or illegal practice.
▶ The actions taken by the organization to improve or eliminate the practice in question.
▶ The organization's efforts to prevent reoccurrence of that practice in the short or long term.
▶ Any disciplinary action(s) taken against corporate officials and employees who were viewed as culpable, too careless or negligent in the matter or who were viewed as not having exercised the proper management responsibility.
▶ Appropriate notices, if applicable, provided to other government agencies.

There is no formulaic answer of what "sufficient" information means with regard to a voluntary disclosure and refund. However, there are some basic guidelines for conducting the initial communications:

1. Focus only on the problem at issue in the disclosure and determinate any dollar impact estimate—these will be a function of the problem under analysis.[3]
2. Do not overstate the impact of corrective actions, especially any present and potential future benefits from those actions.
3. Initiate any related reviews and implement "fixes" to address potential new risks and any existing compliance problems.
4. Consider advising the government that investigations into new risks and new potential problem areas have been or will be started promptly.

It is essential to verify and validate facts rather than simply rely on available documentation. It is often the case that the current information available within the organization may not reflect historical facts or operations.

After identifying the areas to review for the voluntary refund, if any, the organization should determine how to plan and conduct the related review to obtain the necessary information regarding the nature of the improper or questioned practice and the issues involved. This planning and execution of a review is similar to a serious investigation within the organization, and it will vary from organization to organization.[4]

If statistical review or analysis is planned, the organization should use a competent and experienced advisor, and relate the review or analysis to reasonable objectives. Although the OIG suggests using its statistical package, RAT-STATS[5], to estimate the amount of a potential refund, there are other statistical packages or methodologies that may be more appropriate for some reviews and disclosures. Some industry and government representatives do not endorse RAT-STATS because they believe there are better approaches. RAT-STATS has its place, but also has its limitations.

Moreover, if statistical sampling is to be used in connection with a health care voluntary disclosure and refund, the organization should be sure to carefully structure its definitions as well as invest the necessary resources in what here are called "look-ups," alternative procedures, offsets, etc.[6] This is to make the health care sampling results more reasonable.

## Responding Appropriately When a Voluntary Refund Becomes Possible

While the government values a prompt response and quality information, the decision regarding how quickly a health care provider should disclose a potential overpayment

---

3. To try to distinguish between small and inconsequential errors and intentional overbilling, for example, consider this: Clerical or inadvertent billing errors with no apparent pattern are different from intentional "upcoding" and deliberate overbilling.

4. For illustrative material, consider these sources: Wanda Wallace, *Auditing* (3rd ed.), South-Western College Publishing: Cincinnati, OH, 1995; "The Yellow Book," or *Government Auditing Standards*, published by the General Accounting Office for the Comptroller General of the United States—the 1994 edition was amended in May and July of 1999; the American Institute of Certified Public Accountants' *General Auditing Standards*, etc.

5. RAT-STATS is a statistical software that was developed by the Regional Advanced Techniques Staff of the Office of Audit Services of the Office of Inspector General.

6. "Look-ups" are, in essence, inconclusive sample item results for which additional information is needed to draw conclusions. Alternative procedures are "back-up" audit or investigative means of verifying the reasonableness of something.

should be carefully made. The period of time involved and where to make that disclosure can also be relevant. Some disclosures happen slowly, yet some take place very quickly. There is no universally accepted rule regarding the appropriate timing of self-disclosure; each organization's situation is unique. Hasty disclosures are mainly done out of apprehension about the worth of alternative decisions.[7]

A health care provider should establish a policy that provides some sort of "happy medium." That is, the policy allows enough time for the organization to adequately understand the problem before it has to disclose it, but does not require so much time to do so that the disclosure process is unnecessarily delayed.[8] The organization should also avoid conduct that could be misconstrued as an attempt to conceal a problem.[9] A compliance team may also want to carefully consider the source of disclosure information and decide whether information that is received from internal sources (which is easily verifiable) should be treated differently than information received from external sources.

The government[10] may not always know how it wants to handle a voluntary self-disclosure. One of the advantages of taking a serial approach to disclosure is that the organization can help the government focus its concerns, while learning the government's issues. On the other hand, it may be wise for a health care provider to proactively provide feedback to the government about a disclosure area. Once the government has taken a position or has assigned a dollar amount to a situation, it can be much more difficult to convince the government to change its position than it is to proactively work with it to arrive at a mutually agreed-upon position.

Another important factor in preparing a voluntary refund is to keep the organization's media relations department informed, but not actively engaged in the process, or require the department to discuss only the facts. An effective disclosure process is one that does not exaggerate the amount of the voluntary refund or overstate the organization's plan to remedy the problem.[11] A health care provider may wish to study what other organizations have done in similar disclosure situations, with regard to both public relations and the timing of disclosure. However, since disclosure involves a local fact set, it is generally not wise to imitate what other organizations have done.

It is important to bear in mind the United States Sentencing Commission Guidelines, effective since 1991, while a health care provider readies itself for a voluntary disclosure and refund. The Federal Sentencing Guidelines list seven factors on which the effectiveness of the compliance program is evaluated. These factors include whether or not the company:

1. Established compliance policies and procedures for its employees.
2. Assigned high-ranking individuals to oversee the compliance program.
3. Took care not to give known wrongdoers positions involving discretion or authority.
4. Provided training to all employees on its policies and procedures.

---

7. Such apprehension often may be partly related to advice that liability can be effectively held to some reasonable minimum in the presence of potential whistle-blowers. Each case must be evaluated on its own facts and circumstances.

8. It may be helpful to know that health care voluntary disclosures can be made serially.

9. For example, it is unwise for an organization to nonchalantly react to a government query about a billing practice, for the organization does not know what information—analytical, personal, correct or incorrect—the government possesses at the time.

10. The statements in this paragraph could also refer to a carrier or fiscal intermediary.

11. The authors' experience is that moderately and fairly understating planned "cures" is the better course of communication.

5. Took steps to ensure compliance and to detect violations such as monitoring and auditing systems as well as created a mechanism through which employees feel safe and comfortable reporting concerns.
6. Consistently responded to detected violations.
7. Evaluated and modified its programs to try to ensure enhanced prevention and detection of illegality.

Thus, those guidelines recognize the benefit of careful compliance in the federal government's public writing. Use of these factors from the United States Sentencing Guidelines is also a practice in the field to date.

## Deciding to Whom the Disclosure and Refund Should Be Made

Another key consideration in the voluntary self-disclosure and refund process is deciding to whom a health care provider should make its disclosure. Although each situation is different, a health care provider can choose to disclose to the carrier or intermediary, the OIG, the Department of Justice or a combination of these and others.

According to the OIG's *Voluntary Self-Disclosure Protocol* (the Protocol), overpayment or billing errors that do not violate federal criminal, civil or administrative laws do not have to be presented in a special disclosure to the federal government. A health care provider can make such refunds or disclosures directly to a carrier or fiscal intermediary that processes claims on behalf of the CMM or another entity responsible for that particular health care program.

The CMM and the OIG expect providers that participate in the federal health care programs, most notably Medicare and Medicaid, take comprehensive measures to prevent fraudulent or abusive, or both, activities as they relate to the receipt of federal funds. In addition, the OIG also expects federal health care program participants to adequately investigate any potential overpayments and report these to the "appropriate authorities."[12] As indicated elsewhere in this chapter, however, the OIG does not guarantee that a health care provider will receive special treatment or reduced punitive damages for conducting these activities.

If a health care provider is in the process of making a decision to make a disclosure to either the OIG or the Department of Justice, it should choose the entity the organization feels most comfortable approaching regarding its circumstances. Organizations should be aware, however, that the Department of Justice does not officially recognize the OIG's Protocol.[13] Moreover, the OIG may determine that the information contained in a health care provider's disclosure warrants referral to the Department of Justice. Even if a health care provider decides to disclose allegations of fraud to the carrier or fiscal intermediary, the matter still may be referred to the Department of Justice. The carrier or fiscal intermediary does not have the authority to allow a health care provider to avoid criminal or civil prose-

---

12. *Provider Self-Disclosure Protocol,* OIG of the United States Department of Health and Human Services, p. 1. See also *Acting Appropriately in an Organization's Response Once a Voluntary Refund Becomes Possible or Probable* herein.

13. In support of both organizations' views on this difference, much could be written. For the purposes of this book, it is the authors' view that guidance, such as the *Self-Disclosure Protocol,* is helpful to many providers. Moreover, this Protocol is relatively too new [issued October 21, 1998] to be viewed as tested at this time.

cution in the United States—only the Department of Justice can allow a health care provider to avoid prosecution.

## Determining the Appropriate Voluntary Self-Disclosure Protocol

According to the OIG's Protocol, a provider may report matters that "in the provider's reasonable assessment, are potentially violative of federal criminal, civil or administrative laws." However, the *Self-Disclosure Protocol* asks providers to report potential errors "only after an initial assessment substantiates there is a problem with noncompliance with program requirements."[14] Although the Protocol does not impose a time limit by which the erroneous or abusive noncompliant practice should be disclosed, most parties involved in voluntary disclosures and potential refunds place an emphasis on early disclosure.[15]

It is essential to consider the risks associated with self-disclosing errors to the United States government. The government does not provide the same protections for organizations disclosing health care fraud as it does for those disclosing defense contract fraud. This is a technical, as well as an operating, difference that should be remedied in the law and regulations to provide those protections to the health care industry. In addition, reporting to the Office of Inspector General or Department of Justice instead of a carrier or intermediary might predispose a government official to view the matter as one possibly involving intentional or "knowing" false claims. As a result, careful choices are necessary. As indicated earlier, the OIG expressly states in its Protocol that providers should use the Protocol only to report apparent violations of the law.[16, 17, 18] Self-disclosing potential major overbilling errors to the OIG—and specifically, attempting to follow the OIG's Protocol, even though such major errors were inadvertent—can minimize the government's future investigation into a health care provider's daily business activities. By conducting an investigation on its own, a health care provider may avoid an intrusive and thorough federal

---

14.  Shelley R. Slade, "Truth and its Consequences: Should You Voluntarily Disclose Overbillings to Law Enforcement?" *The Health Lawyer* (American Bar Association: Chicago, June 2000) p. 36.

15.  There is a fine line between disclosing too hastily and waiting too long to disclose potential overpayments. An organization has to be comfortable with the process it establishes to gather the relevant facts. The time required to gather all of the relevant facts, however, may be years, after which time the organization may have had multiple claims brought against it by whistleblowers or the government. On the other hand, it is not possible for an organization to gather all the relevant facts in a few days or even a few weeks. The organization, however, should disclose to the government, carrier or fiscal intermediary that the organization is performing a self-audit, and that it will provide periodic information throughout the process. In the authors' view, the ideal voluntary disclosure is performed serially, that is, in a number of steps, over a reasonable period of time.

16.  Slade, *op. cit.*, p. 37

17.  Given its extensive resources, this caveat may well have been an effort to prevent the OIG from being deluged with major and minor billing adjustments (e.g., inadvertent errors) from providers who go to the extreme with communications to their reimbursement sources.

18.  Moreover, circumstances can emerge in which the government feels it has been misled; such a situation can cause the government to be more difficult to deal with than would be expected.

investigation. Federal investigations have a tendency to be overly broad and intrusive, as well as totally outside a health care provider's control. An internal investigation into the same matter may often be more focused, efficient and timely.[19]

The False Claims Act, enacted at the height of the Civil War, is a federal statute that is applicable to entities that contract with and take revenue from the United States government. The False Claims Act was created out of a perceived need for a special law to prosecute the unfortunate conduct of contractors supplying Union forces during the Civil War.[20] The original False Claims Act required a specific demonstration of a contractor's intent to defraud the government to sustain an allegation of a "false" claim. In 1986, Congress significantly amended the False Claims Act to place more accountability on parties contracting with the federal government. The 1986 amendments eased the requirements and now allow a more limited intent or knowledge regarding the submission of false claims to support an allegation of civil fraud case—which is somewhat loosely referred to as the concept of willful negligence or reckless disregard in the health care world. According to the 1986 False Claims Act amendments, when proving an allegation of fraud, the federal government need only show that the defendant had actual knowledge of the false information, or acted in reckless disregard of the truth of that information; proof of specific intent to defraud the government is no longer required under the False Claims Act.

The amendments also increased the penalties for a false claim from $2,000 for each claim to a range of $5,000 to $10,000 for each claim, and increased damages to treble damages in certain situations. However, if the Court finds that a health care provider cooperated with the government to the extent outlined in the Act, the Court may assess no less than twice the amount of damages that the government has sustained. Since the False Claims Act was amended, the government has reported that it has recovered more than $3 billion dollars from government contractors through February 2000.[21]

The 1986 amendments of the False Claims Act, which also increased the financial rewards for whistle-blowers (also referred to as "relators"), may have had the unintended effect of providing a somewhat perverse incentive for individuals involved in, or who have knowledge of, fraudulent activities to inform on their co-conspirators. In amendments to the False Claims Act enacted in 1988, Congress sought to remedy this potential situation by reducing a relator's recovery to zero if the relator "planned and initiated" a violation of the Act. The 1988 amendments set up a "sliding scale" for relator status: Those relators who are convicted of a crime in spite of their whistle-blower status are on one end of the spectrum; on the other end are those relators who have truly uncovered fraud perpetrated by others and have significantly aided the government in the recovery of fraudulent overpayments. The latter relators may be eligible to recover some 25 percent of the government's proceeds.[22]

The Department of Justice issued a Guidance Memorandum in 1998 stating that government attorneys should not allege False Claims Act violations unless reasonable legal and factual predicates have been provided.[23] It is also important for health care providers

19. Slade, *op. cit.*, p. 39

20. The problem reared its head as early as the Revolutionary War.

21. "Justice Department Recovers Over $3 Billion in Whistle-blowers False Claims Act Awards and Settlements," United States Department of Justice press release, February 24, 2000.

22. Stewart M. Gerson, "The False Claims Act Since the 1986 Amendments: Has it Been Worth it? Observations on Enforcement Levels and Trends and Proposals for Improvement," material from the *National Institute on the Civil False Claims Act and Qui Tam Enforcement* (American Bar Association: Chicago, 1998) p. A-10.

to remember that violations of the False Claims Act also can be considered violations of the Social Security Act, which governs much of Medicare and Medicaid.

## Continuing With Improvements to the Compliance Program

As a result of Corporate Integrity Agreements, which providers and the OIG negotiate as part of the settlement of federal health care program investigations, some health care providers have ongoing commitments for compliance in place. A Corporate Integrity Agreement typically lasts three to five years and requires a health care provider to hire a Chief Compliance Officer and appoint a compliance committee, develop written standards and policies for compliance, implement a comprehensive employee training program, establish a plan for voluntary disclosure, and more.

Whether or not a health care provider has a Corporate Integrity Agreement as a result of prior billing and overpayment errors, it is wise for the organization to have a plan for continuing to improve its compliance program. Generally, it is not enough to disclose errors to the appropriate entity (e.g., a government agency, insurer, carrier or intermediary). A health care provider should be able to demonstrate that the senior management team is aware of the problem that gave rise to the voluntary disclosure and refund, and that the organization is trying to prevent those same errors from occurring again by making improvements to its compliance program. The Board of Directors should also be actively and appropriately involved in monitoring corrective actions. Once a health care provider discloses billing errors to the government, the organization's efforts to strengthen its corporate compliance program can help restore its legitimacy as a health care provider participating in federal health care programs. Even for those organizations that do not have compliance problems, it is good business practice to continuously look for ways to strengthen and improve their compliance programs.

## Listening to Reasonable Government Suggestions

A health care organization that is communicating with the federal government—before, during and after a voluntary self-disclosure and refund—should be willing to incorporate the government's suggestions for improvements into the organization's compliance program. This willingness may not only serve to facilitate a health care provider's settlement negotiations with the government, but also may serve as another signal to the government that the organization is thoughtfully, effectively and openly addressing compliance issues. This, in turn, may boost the health care organization's credibility with the government and may facilitate any future negotiations or even disclosures. Moreover, it is essential to remember that the federal government has more experience analyzing disclosed overpayment errors than do most organizations presenting such differences and error corrections. Thus, a health care provider should consider reasonable suggestions for improvement provided by government officials.

---

23. See also Deputy Attorney General Eric H. Holder's guidance memorandum issued to all U.S. Attorneys General June 3, 1998, regarding prosecuting providers under the False Claims Act.

## Ensuring That Compliance Personnel Have the Capabilities to Do a Good Job

During its communications with the government, a health care provider should have confidence in its compliance personnel to effectively represent the organization and to act in its best interests. Once a voluntary disclosure and refund has become a possibility, any interactions with the government should not overstate the organization's compliance capabilities or plans for correcting the disclosed problem. It is important that compliance personnel have sufficient information to make an accurate disclosure to the government, and that they accurately depict the magnitude of the problem and any actions underway to correct it. If compliance personnel attempt to conceal or inaccurately present a compliance problem, and a federal investigation uncovers these misrepresentations, the organization's credibility or trustworthiness could be irreparably harmed.

## Continuing to Advocate Contractual and Regulatory Clarifications

Many overpayment and billing errors are often linked to complex and unclear government regulations. One area in which a health care organization can use communications with the government to improve its compliance environment is to advocate for contractual and regulatory clarifications. A health care provider can also use a compliance situation as an opportunity to highlight a complex billing regulation—one specific to the disclosure situation.

## Continuing Education and Training

The experience of the voluntary disclosure situation will undoubtedly provide many opportunities for continuing education and training. Compliance personnel will be responsible for training health care line and staff personnel on how to correct the disclosed error or refund problem. Effective training is a health care provider's best way to disseminate information and test employees' comprehension of the subject matter. Ongoing internal training signals to the government that a health care provider is serious about compliance and that it recognizes the importance of training in maintaining the organization's compliance with applicable rules and regulations and achieving its organizational goals.

*The views presented are based on the authors' experience as consultants to the health care industry; neither Catherine Sreckovich nor Alan Peterson is an attorney.*

# CHAPTER 7

# Medicaid Program Provider Self-Audits

## Gregory A. Brodek and Emmy S. Monahan

The Medicaid program is the result of legislation enacted in 1965, which provided for state-administered and federally monitored financing of medical services to eligible needy individuals.[1] Since states are given wide discretion with respect to the amount, duration and scope of Medicaid coverage, no two state Medicaid programs are alike. Medicaid's annual national budget has expanded significantly from almost $4 billion dollars in 1968 to more than $130 billion in 1993.[2] The Department of Health and Human Services' Office of Inspector General (OIG) estimates that fraud and abuse in the Medicaid program cost the government at least $653 million a year.[3]

In response to the increase in suspected fraud and abuse against Medicaid and Medicare, Congress passed legislation to halt the criminal activity against the two programs. This legislation, signed into law by President Carter on October 25, 1977, is titled the Medicare/Medicaid Anti-Fraud and Abuse Amendments, Pub. Law 95-142. The Amendments made federal funding available to states that establish a Medicaid fraud and abuse control unit.[4] The function of the Medicaid fraud and abuse control units is to conduct statewide investigations and prosecutions of applicable state laws regarding any and all aspects of fraud in connection with Medicaid.[5] According to the OIG, in fiscal year 1999, the Medicaid fraud and abuse control units recovered more than $88 million and obtained 886 convictions.[6]

---

1. Office of Inspector General, U.S. Department of Health and Human Services, *State Medicaid Fraud Control Units Annual Report for Fiscal Years 1997/1998/1999*, at 2, at http://www.oig.hhs.gov/oi/mfcu/index.htm [hereinafter OIG Annual Report]

2. Health Care Financing Administration, U.S. Department of Health and Human Services, Medicaid Bureau Fraud and Abuse Information, at 1, at http://www.hcfa.gov/medicaid/mbfraud.htm [hereinafter Medicaid Bureau Fraud and Abuse Information]

3. OIG Annual Report, at 2

4. *Id.*

5. The units are also charged with the investigation of complaints of the abuse and neglect of patients in medical facilities receiving Medicaid payments. 42 U.S.C. §§ 1396b(q)(3) and (4) (2000); see also 42 C.F.R. § 1007.11 (2000).

6. OIG Annual Report, at 6

Additionally, federal regulation requires Medicaid agencies to implement a surveillance and utilization control program that safeguards against unnecessary or inappropriate use of Medicaid services and assesses the quality of those services.[7] A vital part of this program is the state surveillance and utilization control units (SURs), which process information on medical services to guide Medicaid program managers. In addition, the SURs are responsible for the identification of health care providers and suppliers (collectively referred to as "providers") suspected of committing fraud against the Medicaid program, and the reporting of all cases of suspected provider fraud to the state Medicaid fraud and abuse control units.[8]

Public enforcement efforts have been significantly expanded with the passage of the Health Insurance Portability and Accountability Act of 1996 (HIPAA), Pub. Law 104-191, which, for the first time, provided generous appropriations for fraud control. HIPAA established, among other things, a fraud and abuse control program that requires the Department of Health and Human Services and the Department of Justice to coordinate federal, state and local health care law enforcement activities, provide guidance to providers on fraudulent practices, and establish a national data bank to receive and report final adverse actions against providers.[9]

The emphasis on combating fraud and abuse has led to a drastic increase in the number of investigations, prosecutions and civil enforcement proceedings. During the six-month period ending March 31, 2000, the OIG reported 1,278 exclusions from the federal health care programs, 205 convictions and 198 civil actions.[10] In addition, more than $968 million were returned as a result of OIG investigations during this same period.[11]

The increase in public enforcement efforts is motivating providers to turn to compliance programs as a first step in reducing their exposure to civil and criminal liability.[12] One of the essential components of a compliance plan is a monitoring and auditing system, which requires the provider to review its claim development and submission process to ensure compliance with applicable laws and regulations relating to Medicare, Medicaid and other federal health care programs.

In addition to self-audits initiated by providers as part of the implementation of their compliance programs, providers may conduct self-audits in connection with investigations led by government agencies into overpayments under the Medicaid program.[13] North Car-

---

7. 42 U.S.C. § 1396a(a)(61); 42 C.F.R. § 456.3

8. 42 C.F.R. § 455.21

9. U.S. Department of Health and Human Services, HHS Fact Sheet, at 2 (March 2000), at http://www.hhs.gov/news/press/2000pres/20000309a.html

10. OIG, U.S. Department of Health and Human Services, Semiannual Report October 1, 1999–March 31, 2000, at i

11. *Id*. at 73

12. In addition, more and more providers are required to implement a compliance program as part of a corporate integrity agreement reached with the government.

13. According to the National Fraud and Abuse Team and Center for Medicaid and State Operations, extending an opportunity to providers to perform a self-audit has proven to be a valuable tool in connection with seeking ways to improve a state's surveillance and utilization review practices. This conclusion was reached in connection with a case that involved incorrect billing by certified nurse practitioners for anesthesia services using units set for one minute, instead of 15 minutes. Eighty providers who billed for more than 16 units per claim were selected for review and each provider was sent a letter extending an opportunity to perform a self-audit for a five-year period. Ninety-nine percent of the providers participated, allowing the state to recover approximately $531,000 within four months. National Fraud and Abuse Team and Center for Medicaid and State Operations, Health Care Financing Administration, *Guidance and Best Practices Relating to the States' Surveillance and Utilization Review Functions*, at 15.

olina, for example, launched a self-audit plan in 1999 under which providers conduct their own investigations into possible billing errors and voluntarily repay the state.[14] Since the beginning of 2000, North Carolina has recovered approximately $1.2 million in Medicaid overpayments due to billing mistakes.[15] In May 2000, the state of Maine's SUR sent a letter to all physicians, suppliers and other providers requesting them to conduct an audit of their own records to ascertain whether they had received any overpayments in the last five years that had not been returned.[16, 17] In the same letter, Maine's SUR announced that it would contract with a private vendor to pursue recovery of any overpayments.[18]

This chapter focuses on self-audits performed in connection with a government investigation for Medicaid overpayments, and discusses (1) the definition of a self-audit, (2) the authority of the states to request that providers conduct self-audits, (3) the self-auditing methodology, (4) the benefits and risks of self-audits, (5) the state of Maine's audit initiative and (6) the tax consequences of involuntary repayment of overpayment amounts previously received.

## What Is a Self-Audit?

In its simplest terms, a self-audit is a formal examination performed by a person or entity of their accounts or financial situation. In the health care context, a self-audit generally includes a review of the provider's bills and medical records to ensure that claim submissions accurately reflect the services provided; in turn, this ensures the provider's reimbursement is accurate and consistent with the applicable laws and regulations relating to whatever government health care program to which the claim was submitted.

The individuals involved in self-audits would ideally include those people in charge of billing and medically trained professionals. Self-audits may be used to determine whether (1) bills are accurately coded and accurately reflect the services or items furnished as documented in the medical records, (2) documentation is complete, (3) services or items provided are reasonable and necessary and (4) any incentives for unnecessary services or items are present.[19]

---

14. "North Carolina Recovers Medicaid Overpayments," 9 BNA's Health Law Reporter 1065 (2000)

15. *Id.*

16. Letter from Marc Fecteau, Manager, State of Maine, Department of Human Services, Surveillance and Utilization Review Unit to Maine Medicaid Providers (May 22, 2000) (on file with author) [hereinafter Maine Letter].

17. Twenty-eight different types of providers, ranging from hospitals, dentists, and physicians to social workers, notified the SUR of having received overpayments, allowing the State of Maine to recoup approximately $504,497. Overpayments were due to, among other reasons, double billing, lack of documentation and mathematical errors. Letter from Marc Fecteau, Manager, State of Maine, Department of Human Services, Surveillance and Utilization Review Unit to Gregory A. Brodek (October 31, 2000) (on file with author).

18. Maine Letter

19. OIG, U.S. Department of Health and Human Services, *The Office of Inspector General Compliance Program Guidance for Individual and Small Group Physician Practices*, at 7 (September 2000)

## Authority of States to Request a Self-Audit

There appears to be no question that the states have the power to conduct compliance audits. Federal law specifically requires that state plans "provide that the records of any entity participating in the plan and providing services reimbursable on a cost-related basis will be audited as the Secretary determines to be necessary to insure that proper payments are made under the plan. . . ."[20] Additionally, federal regulation requires that Medicaid agencies implement a surveillance and utilization control program that safeguards against unnecessary or inappropriate use of Medicaid services and assesses the quality of services.[21] Federal regulation also explicitly directs that a "Medicaid agency must assure appropriate audit of records if payment is based on costs of services or on a fee plus cost of materials."[22] In addition to federal law and regulations, state regulation typically contains a provision providing for the state to conduct audits.[23] Similarly, the Medicaid participating provider agreement generally contains a provision allowing the Medicaid agency to review all of a provider's records.[24]

Thus, it is clear that, pursuant to both federal and state regulation as well as the provider agreement, a state has the authority and obligation to conduct audits. In doing so, it has the power to request that providers make their records available or furnish the state with copies of relevant documents. However, there is neither federal nor state authority to require that a provider conduct a self-audit. Inasmuch as federal and state regulators saw the necessity to specifically grant the Medicaid agency the authority to conduct audits, it does not have the authority to shift that responsibility and burden to the provider.

## Self-Auditing Methodology

A common dilemma providers face is deciding what to include in the self-audit. Providers should assess their environment for specific risk areas. One good source of information is the Medicaid Bureau Fraud and Abuse Information, which lists a variety of activities that the Centers for Medicare and Medicaid Services (CMS, formerly the Health Care Financing Administration) has identified as the "most common rip-offs."[25] According to CMS, the most common rip-offs include:

▶ Billing for phantom patient visits
▶ Billing for goods or services not provided, or old items as new
▶ Billing for more hours than there are in a day
▶ Billing for medically unnecessary testing
▶ Paying kickbacks in exchange for referrals
▶ Charging personal expenses to Medicaid
▶ Inflating the bills for services or goods provided

---

20. 42 U.S.C. § 1396a(a)(42)
21. 42 C.F.R. § 456.3
22. 42 C.F.R. § 447.202
23. See, e.g., Code Me. R. § 10-144 Ch. 101 ("Maine Medical Assistance Manual") Ch. I § 1.12.
24. See, e.g., Medicaid/Maine Health Program Provider/Supplier Agreement (on file with author).
25. Medicaid Bureau Fraud and Abuse Information, at 1

▶ Concealing ownership of related companies
▶ Falsifying credentials and double billing

Self-audits conducted in conjunction with government investigations into Medicaid over-payments essentially consist of two methodologies. Under the first, the provider will initiate an audit into its own billing practices to determine whether accurate claims were submitted to Medicaid and to make certain that it has otherwise complied with applicable laws and regulations relating to this program. Under the second self-audit methodology, the provider will self-audit the types of claims identified by the Medicaid agency as potentially involving billing errors.

When structuring a self-audit under the first methodology, providers should limit the audit to specific areas in which they know overpayments have been received to protect themselves against civil and criminal liability. In addition, careful consideration should be given to the sampling technique to be used (e.g., 100 percent, random). By increasing the sample size, the provider may unnecessarily subject itself to additional repayment obligations that a smaller sample would not have allowed the provider to identify.[26]

## Benefits and Risks

One of the benefits of conducting a self-audit is that the provider is able to control and manage the audit process, thereby lessening disruption within the organization. In addition, the process requires the provider to analyze its internal policies and procedures related to its billing practices, the results of which may prove to be of assistance in devising a compliance program and improving billing practices.[27] From a state's perspective, the approach minimizes agency time and resources, thereby maximizing the recovery per agency hour invested. In addition, the provider's investigation may reveal a more extensive problem than the Medicaid agency is aware of, which could result in an even larger repayment. Similarly, a self-audit approach permits the Medicaid agency to obtain information about problems it may otherwise not have knowledge about. The results of a provider's self-audit also may be used by the Medicaid agency to identify other providers with similar problems.[28]

Self-audits are not, however, without substantial risks for providers. For example, there is no guarantee that conducting a self-audit and disclosing the receipt of any Medicaid overpayments will mitigate the possibility of further review by the SUR or Medicaid fraud and abuse control unit in any current or future investigations. Self-audits may also not affect the government's ability to pursue criminal, civil or administrative remedies or to obtain additional damages, penalties or fines for the matters that are the subject of the self-audit.[29] The government has been unwilling to provide "a meaningful guarantee of amnesty" to providers that are willing to voluntarily report program abuses.[30] In addition, self-

---

26. Daniel R. Roach, "Primer on Compliance Programs," in American Health Lawyers Association *Fundamentals of Health Law* (2000).

27. "Physician Payment IG to Audit all Hospital Academic Institutions Under PATH, Official Says," 5 BNA's *Health Law Reporter* 1119 (1996).

28. Program Integrity, Division of Medical Assistance, North Carolina Department of Human Resources, Provider Self-Auditing, at 1 (on file with author) [hereinafter Provider Self-Auditing].

29. Provider Self-Auditing at 2; DHHS, OIG, Publication of the OIG's *Provider Self-Disclosure Protocol*, 63 Fed. Reg. 58,400.

30. Michael M. Mustokoff et al., "Full Amnesty Could Encourage Provider Self-Disclosure" (July 31, 2000), at 7, at http://www.duanemorris.com/publications/printer/ppub81.html

audits could lead to a whistle blower or *qui tam* action, and trigger repayment obligations that may otherwise not exist.[31] For example, federal law requires a provider to disclose any knowledge of an event affecting the provider's initial or continued right to any such benefit or payment.[32] Under this provision even simple billing errors, which may not have any criminal intent, can become criminal if the provider does not report the error once it becomes aware of it.

## Case Study of State of Maine Audit Initiative

### Audit Initiative

As noted above, the SUR in Maine requested that all providers participating in the Medicaid program conduct a self-audit to ascertain whether they had received any overpayments that had not been returned in the last five years. In doing so, the SUR indicated that the Maine Bureau of Medical Services (the Bureau) "is acutely aware that Medicaid providers have identified and determined receipt of Medicaid overpayments but have failed to report these instances or to reimburse the Medicaid Program; many have simply never reconciled their debts to Medicaid."[33]

In its efforts to recover overpayments, the Bureau issued a request for proposals (RFP) in April 2000 for entities willing to undertake an audit of all payments made by the Bureau to Medicaid providers over the past five years to identify and assist the state in recouping overpayments.[34] Public Consulting Group, Inc. (PCG), in conjunction with IBM as a subcontractor, was selected by the Bureau to perform the audits.

Under the audit process, PCG will not necessarily be required to review all relevant and necessary patient charts and records required to verify alleged overpayments; instead, it may perform a selective review of charts.[35] PCG has the authority to reach a settlement with the provider, provided the amount of the settlement is not less than the Medicaid payment amount.[36] PCG will receive base compensation equal to 25 percent of the total amount of overpayments recouped on behalf of the state of Maine (i.e., net of the federal government's share of the recovery).[37] Significantly, underpayments identified by PCG will not be communicated to the provider whose claims are being reviewed.

The Maine Medical Association has developed a bill, L.D. 246, An Act to Ensure Appropriate Audit Procedures, sponsored by Representative Arthur F. Mayo, III, that would preclude the Department from conducting the audit in the manner contemplated.[38] Specifically,

---

31. "Physician Payment IG to Audit all Hospital Academic Institutions Under PATH, Official Says," 5 BNA's Health Law Reporter 1118 (1996)

32. 42 U.S.C. § 1320a-7b(a)(3)

33. Maine Letter

34. Request for Proposals, State of Maine, Department of Human Services, Bureau of Medical Services, at 3 (Apr. 2000) [hereinafter Maine RFP]

35. Proposal to Provide Fraud and Abuse Detection Services for the State of Maine, Public Consulting Group, Inc., at II-15 (2000)

36. Maine RFP, at 14

37. The Maine RFP contemplates the ability of the outside vendor to receive additional compensation for exceeding performance standards, but reference, if any, to this in PCG's response has been redacted.

38. L.D. 246, An Act to Ensure Appropriate Audit Procedures, at 2 (March 2001).

When conducting audits pursuant to this section, the Department shall not engage a private vendor to conduct the audit or base the auditor's compensation on a percentage of the alleged overpayment amount. The Department must disclose to the public any mathematical algorithm used in performance of any audit. This subsection applies retroactively to January 1, 2000.[39]

The Health and Human Services Committee has recommended passage of L.D. 246.[40] On April 18, 2001, the Office of Fiscal and Program Review submitted the fiscal note information on the bill, estimating its costs at $9,000,593 in fiscal year 2001–2002 and $4,830,217 in fiscal year 2002–2003.[41] The fiscal impact of L.D. 246 will likely impede its passage, as "[i]t will be difficult to reduce the fiscal note enough to remove the bill from the Appropriations Table[.]"[42] The Maine Medical Association, along with Representative Mayo, is expected to make legislators aware of provider opposition to the audit initiative and to seek "strong roll call votes" on the bill in the Maine Senate and the Maine House of Representatives.[43]

## Issues Raised by Audit Initiative

Maine's audit initiative gives rise to several issues that should be of particular concern to providers. While the state has the power to audit, it appears that such power is not being exercised in a manner that is reasonably related to the purpose for which the audit is being conducted—that is, to identify overpayments. The audit initiative is certain to identify alleged overpayments. However, given the potential lack of medical record review in all instances where such a review may be necessary to determine whether an overpayment has occurred, it is not inconceivable that the audit initiative is not reasonably designed to accomplish its stated purpose.

The initiative could affect the state's relationship with the providers that participate in the Medicaid program. Based upon the generally low reimbursement rates being paid to providers for rendering services and supplies to the indigent population, providers may not be willing to incur the expense of having to defend every allegation of overpayment that might be brought in connection with the initiative. Consequently, a provider may decide to discontinue participation in the program.

In addition, the ability of the state to enter into a contingency fee arrangement with PCG seems inconsistent with the purpose of the audit initiative. Notwithstanding the foregoing, the Maine statutes authorize the Department of Human Services (the Department) to enter into contracts with health care service entities for the provision, financing, management and delivery of health care services to carry out its programs and to utilize performance-based contracts.[44] Even though the provision recommending the Department to utilize performance-based contracts is not directly related to the audit process, it is illustrative of the state's ability to engage in such relationships.

As noted above, while there seems to be no question that the states have the power to conduct compliance audits, it is not entirely clear whether the state of Maine could look

---

39. *Id.* at 1–2

40  Maine Medical Association, Eighteenth Weekly Legislative Update, at 4 (May 18, 2001) [hereinafter MMA Legislative Update]

41. Office of Fiscal and Program Review, Maine State Legislature, Fiscal Note Information for L.D. 246, at 1 (Apr. 18, 2001)

42. MMA Legislative Update, at 4

43. *Id.*

44. Me. Rev. Stat. Ann. tit. 22, §§ 12-A and 3173 (West 2000)

back five years for purposes of auditing and recouping overpayments. Maine's regulation does not contain a statute of limitations that directly applies to recouping overpayments.[45] Although the state may claim otherwise, the section providing for a five-year records retention period would not constitute a period of limitation for recoupment purposes. Given the regulation's silence as to a limitation period for recoupment of overpayments and the federal government's financial participation in the Medicaid program,[46] the applicable period is arguably governed by that provided under the federal Medicare program. Under the Medicare program, there is a four-year limitation imposed on reopening an intermediary's or carrier's decision to pay a claim, except in cases where there has been fraud or similar fault.[47] Under this approach, the state would be precluded from going back five years, possibly even for audit purposes, unless it can show suspected fraud.

While the Medicaid agency or PCG will look back five years for overpayments, the audit initiative would limit providers to a significantly shorter period. Under the Maine regulation, the provider would have 120 days from the date he, she or it received the remittance statement to request a review of that payment if he, she or it believes an underpayment has been received for covered services rendered.[48] There is no similar limitation, however, in the event the Medicaid agency determines that, as the result of an audit, an underpayment has been made to a provider.[49]

Finally, although the state's RFP and PCG's response address the recovery process, there remains a great deal of uncertainty as to how the audits will actually be conducted. Ordinarily, a provider will receive a letter from the SUR that summarizes its findings, including supporting documentation,[50] and outlines the provider's rights when an alleged overpayment is identified. Upon receipt of such a letter, a provider has three options: (1) request a meeting with the SUR,[51] (2) request an informal review by the Director of the Bureau (Director) or (3) repay the entire amount of the alleged overpayment (either by check, set-off from future payments, or in cases of hardship, some other agreed upon payment arrangement).[52] A provider's failure to contest an overpayment within 30 days from receipt of the SUR's letter notifying a provider of the perceived overpayment will constitute the provider's agreement to the findings made by the Bureau.[53]

If an alleged overpayment is not contested within 30 days, or other repayment arrangements have not been agreed to by the Bureau, the Bureau will recoup the overpayment by reducing some or all of the provider's reimbursement due on pending and/or future claims.[54] State law allows the Bureau to implement recoupment procedures following

---

45. Maine Medical Assistance Manual Ch. I §§ 1.10.2 and 1.12

46. *Id*. § 1.18-2B

47. Medicare Intermediary Manual § 3708; Medicare Carriers Manual §§ 7102, 7103 and 7106

48. Maine Medical Assistance Manual Ch. I § 1.10-1

49. *Id*.

50. In notifying providers of alleged overpayments, the SUR has historically provided documentation that identifies the patient(s) to which the payment(s) relate, date(s) of service, payment(s) made, amount of overpayment(s) and reason why the payment(s) has(have) been determined to constitute an "overpayment."

51. Although not required, the SUR has historically been willing to meet with providers and review the findings that have been made and, if supported by evidence produced by the provider, reconsider its decision to consider certain payments as overpayments.

52. Maine Medical Assistance Manual Ch. I §§ 1.10-2 and 1.19

53. *Id*.

54. Maine Medical Assistance Manual Ch. I § 1.19

the informal review phase if the decision is in favor of the Department.[55] A provider wishing to contest a finding of overpayment must first request an informal review by the Director or his designee.[56] If a provider is dissatisfied with the informal review process, the provider may request an administrative hearing.

Significantly, recently proposed revisions to the Maine regulation would clearly limit those matters that may be reviewed at the administrative hearing and "all subsequent appeal proceedings" to those issues raised during the informal review.[57] As a result of these proposed changes, it may be imperative for a provider to be represented by counsel at even the informal review phase of the appeal process. If an administrative hearing is requested, the hearing officer will issue a written decision and, if unfavorable, the provider may appeal the administrative decision to the Superior Court. The process from informal review to the Superior Court is not fast, and given the anticipated number of audits that will likely be completed and contested, one can only expect that the review process will be even slower.

## Tax Consequences of Involuntary Repayment of Amounts Previously Received

The repayment of overpayments made to the provider raises the question of whether the provider is able to obtain federal income tax relief. When a provider is required to repay an item that was included in gross income for a prior taxable year(s) because it appeared that the provider had an unrestricted right to that item, the provider is not permitted to amend the return for the year in which the payment was received and thereby claim a refund of an overpayment of tax for that year together with appropriate interest. Instead, the provider is entitled to compute its tax liability for the taxable year in which the repayment is made under the provisions of section 1341 of the Internal Revenue Code of 1986, as amended, provided the following requirements are satisfied:

1. An item was included in gross income for prior taxable year(s) because it appeared that the provider had an unrestricted right to the item.[58]
2. A deduction, whether ordinary or capital, is allowable for the taxable year of repayment of the item by the provider because it was established after close of the prior taxable year(s) in which the item was received that the provider did not have an unrestricted right to the item or a portion of such item, but only when the determination is based on facts or events in the year of receipt, not on subsequent developments occurring after that year (e.g., a change of law).
3. The amount of the deduction must exceed $3,000.[59]

---

55. Id. If the Bureau were to commence the recoupment process prior to the provider exhausting all his appeal rights, such practice may significantly deter the willingness of providers to appeal the Bureau's or PCG's findings. Additionally, implementing such a policy may result in providers simply electing to opt out of the Medicaid program entirely.

56. *Id.*

57. Proposed Rule: Maine Medical Assistance Manual Ch. I § 1.21

58. Illegally obtained amounts (e.g., embezzled funds, fraudulently or falsely claimed amounts) would not be eligible.

59. 26 U.S.C. § 1341(a)

If the above three requirements are satisfied, the tax of the provider for the taxable year of the repayment is the lesser of:[60]

4. The tax for the taxable year computed by taking a deduction for the repayment
5. An amount equal to (i) the tax for the taxable year computed without taking a deduction for repayment, minus (ii) the decrease in tax for the prior taxable year(s) that would result solely from the exclusion of the repaid item (or portion thereof) from the provider's gross income for such prior taxable year(s).[61]

If the computation of the tax for the taxable year, determined by taking into account the deduction for the repayment (i.e., under (a), above), results in a net operating loss for the taxable year of the repayment, the net operating loss is to be carried back under the rules of section 172 of the Internal Revenue Code and treated as a net operating loss in each of the two taxable years preceding the taxable year of repayment.[62] If the aggregate decrease in tax for the taxable year(s) to which the net operating loss is carried back is greater than the excess of the amount determined under (b) above, then the tax imposed for the taxable year is the amount determined under (a) above. In that case, the decrease in tax for the taxable year(s) to which the net operating loss was carried back shall be treated as an overpayment of tax for the carryback year(s) and shall be refunded or credited as an overpayment for such taxable year(s).[63]

If the decrease in tax for the taxable year determined under (b) exceeds the income tax imposed for the taxable year (computed without any deduction for the repayment), that excess shall be considered to be a payment of tax on the last day prescribed by law for the payment of tax for the taxable year of repayment and shall be refunded or credited in the same manner as if it were an overpayment for such taxable year.[64]

In any case in which the exclusion referred to in (b)(ii) above results in a net operating loss or capital loss for the prior taxable year(s), then, for purposes of computing the decrease in tax for the prior taxable year(s), such loss shall be carried back and carried over as provided in section 172 or 1212 of the Internal Revenue Code, except that no carryover beyond the taxable year of repayment shall be taken into account.[65]

Thus, a repayment by a provider of excess amounts it received in prior years under the Medicaid program, based upon claims that it believed to be correct when submitted, causing the provider to include the excess payments in gross income for those years because it appeared that the provider had an unrestricted right to such payments, will result, when repayment is made in a subsequent year, in the application of the relief provided under section 1341 to the repayments made by the provider, provided the repayments are required by law and not voluntary on the part of the provider, and the amount of the repayments exceeds $3,000.

The determination of the precise manner in which the relief provided under section 1341 will apply to the provider can only be made after an examination of all the relevant facts, including all the items necessary to prepare its tax return for the year in which repayment is made and all the tax returns for each year in which it received the excess Medicaid payments that generate the provider's liability for repayment of those amounts. Only then can the relatively complicated rules summarized above be properly applied with confidence.

---

60. The application of section 1341 of the Internal Revenue Code in the year of repayment is mandatory. 26 U.S.C. § 1341(a) (the flush language appearing immediately after subsection (a)(3)).
61. 26 U.S.C. § 1341(a)(4), (5)
62. 26 U.S.C. § 1341(b)(4)(A)
63. 26 C.F.R. § 1.1341-1(b)(1)(iii)
64. 26 U.S.C. § 1341(b)(1)
65. 26 U.S.C. § 1341(b)(4)(B)

PART

# Mandatory Compliance Monitoring and Auditing

# Corporate Integrity Agreement Negotiations

## Ronald L. Wisor, Jr.

I f a company, facility, agency or practice is ever involved in a federal health care fraud investigation, unless it is wholly exonerated, a Corporate Integrity Agreement (CIA) with the Office of Inspector General of the Department of Health and Human Services (OIG) will be a likely result of the investigation. The OIG began to include CIAs in the government's civil settlements of health care fraud cases in the mid-1990s.

Today, such agreements have become the norm in the settlement of cases involving allegations of false claims or other wrongdoing for which the OIG has authority to exclude providers from participation in Medicare and other federal health care programs. In fact, the legal basis relied upon by the OIG for imposing a CIA is that it is a substitute for exclusion. The theory is that without the CIA, the OIG would not be able to trust the provider to participate in the federal health care programs and, but for the CIA, the OIG's only recourse under such circumstances would be exclusion.

The OIG has now entered into more than 400 CIAs with virtually all types of health care providers. The purpose of this chapter is to provide some helpful tips on successfully negotiating a CIA with the OIG, an entity with bargaining power that is immeasurably aided by its discretionary exclusion authority. Since no provider organization voluntarily seeks to enter into a CIA, it is important that the organization negotiate a CIA it can tolerate for up to five years, and sometimes longer.

## Establish Credibility Early

The process of establishing credibility should have begun long before an organization enters into negotiations with the government. This may be done through the development of a well established voluntary compliance program with a proven track record. Indeed, an established, effective and credible compliance program should provide the leverage necessary to help an organization successfully negotiate with the OIG. This means having:

▶ A compliance officer who has clout with senior management, and who is able to effectively deal with the Chief Executive Officer and other senior managers, as well as the billing office and sales staff.

▶ A comprehensive Code of Conduct that emphasizes the importance of compliance, and documentation that shows it is properly disseminated to all employees.

▶ A structured training program and written evidence that every employee receives initial training and annual retraining.

▶ Written policies and procedures compiled so they can easily be shared with the OIG.

▶ Evidence of an annual self-auditing plan, including documentation that overpayments are routinely refunded.

There have been cases where companies with an effective compliance program have been able to settle fraud cases with the government with only a promise that they maintain their current program—that is, without a CIA. These cases are exceedingly rare, though, and most providers can expect a CIA with any fraud or false claims settlement.

The success a health care organization has with negotiating a CIA, however, primarily will be a function of how effective its past compliance efforts have been. If the organization cannot demonstrate that it already has a credible program, then it is unlikely the OIG will agree to any provisions that depart from its standard agreement.

## Don't Put Off CIA Negotiations Until the End

Putting off CIA negotiations is a common mistake. Companies and their lawyers will spend countless hours negotiating the finer details of the settlement agreement—95 percent of which is standard and nonnegotiable—while giving no serious thought to the terms of a CIA the provider may have to live with for the next three, five, or in some cases, eight years.

There are generally three scenarios that explain why CIA negotiations are not taken as seriously as they should be. First, management assumes the CIA is the same as a compliance program, and since they already have one of those, the CIA is no big deal. Or, second, management assumes, or is told by Counselor others, that CIAs are nonnegotiable, so they do not attempt to negotiate the CIA. Or, third, management (or Counsel) simply fails to plan ahead and does not leave enough time for meaningful discussion of the CIA before the settlement must be finalized.

The first two assumptions are wrong and, hopefully, this chapter will help readers avoid the fate suffered by those providers in the third scenario. Although the *U.S. Sentencing Guidelines* and the OIG's model *Compliance Program Guidance* are the foundation for CIAs, over time CIAs have grown longer, more expansive and more detailed as the OIG has gained experience negotiating them. Through the CIA, the OIG prescribes certain policies and procedures that could have a significant impact on how an organization conducts its business for years to come. CIAs also require auditing, which must be performed by an independent review organization (IRO) and must be based upon auditing protocols and plans established by the OIG. In many cases, these IRO audits could be more costly to the provider than its settlement with the government. Moreover, if there is any doubt regarding the reliability of the IRO audits, the OIG can require additional auditing at the company's expense.

There are a variety of penalties that may be imposed for violating the terms of a CIA, including a series of per diem fines, which typically range from $1,000–$2,500 per day depending upon the seriousness of the deficiency, and the ultimate penalty—exclusion from federal health care programs—for the most serious violations.

In short, there are plenty of incentives for starting the CIA review process early. Once settlement discussions get serious, the company should begin to assemble its CIA negotiating team. Once an agreement in principle is reached on the settlement, the provider should contact the OIG to start working in earnest on the CIA.

## Involve Company Personnel in the Negotiations

Another common mistake made by providers is to involve only lawyers in the CIA negotiations. While an experienced health care attorney is an essential member of the negotiating team, lawyers in general—and outside lawyers in particular—are not familiar with the company's infrastructure, its current policies and procedures, the detailed rules and regulations that apply to the company's daily operations or how its industry sector conducts business. This is extremely important, especially as the CIA provisions relating to mandatory policies and procedures become increasingly elaborate. Not only do knowledgeable company insiders help to keep the OIG's expectations realistic, but it is also an opportunity for them to educate the OIG about the industry and the detailed regulations that already apply to the company.

Also, it is essential that the compliance officer take a leading role in the negotiations. This serves three important purposes. First, the compliance officer is generally the person most familiar with the company's current compliance program and, therefore, he or she is usually the person best able to comment on how the CIA should be structured in order to accommodate the program. Second, through his or her involvement in negotiating the details of the CIA, the compliance officer will learn both what is required by the CIA and the OIG's underlying rationale and expectations with regard to those requirements. Third, involvement in the CIA negotiations provides the compliance officer with the opportunity to establish credibility and begin a dialogue with the OIG.

## Use a Lawyer Who Has Experience Negotiating CIAs

Using an experienced lawyer may seem self-evident, but it needs to be said. The following story will help illustrate this point.

A number of years ago, I received a phone call from a lawyer who was negotiating the settlement of a false claims case with the government on behalf of a hospital. The lawyer was a criminal attorney with a very prestigious firm, but was not experienced in health care matters. He asked if I could review the settlement agreement to see if there were any health care issues that jumped out at me.

After reviewing the documents and providing a few brief comments on the settlement agreement, I proceeded to list a number of serious problems with the draft CIA the OIG was asking the hospital to sign. About five minutes into my litany about how impossible it would be for a small community hospital to comply with the requirements of the draft document, the hospital's lawyer cut me off. "You have to pick your battles," I recall him saying, "and my impression is that these CIAs are all just standard, boiler-plate stuff." He thanked me for my time and indicated he was going to focus his efforts on obtaining an extended payment period on the settlement amount.

I still wonder whether that hospital was ever able to get every physician with staff privileges to attend seven hours of compliance training, or whether it was able to comply with about a half dozen other difficult provisions in the CIA that, if compliance was not achieved, would result in fines of $2,500 per day and program exclusion.

This happens more often than one might think. In many cases, companies make the seemingly logical assumption that the lawyer who represented them in the government investigation is also in the best position to negotiate the CIA with the OIG. This may or may not be true. Many very fine defense lawyers who have been able to achieve excellent results with the local United States attorney's office may have no knowledge of, or experience with, the OIG or CIAs. In those situations, providers may want to consider retaining the assistance of a firm that has experience negotiating CIAs, knows the OIG attorneys with whom it will be negotiating, and is familiar with what issues are open for discussion and what realistically can be achieved through negotiations.

## Be Realistic

If a company is entering into a CIA, chances are the government has identified some problems in the past with how it was conducting business. Even if management does not agree, certainly the OIG approaches negotiations with that in mind. As a provider enters negotiations with the government, it is not the time to proclaim innocence or to resist those standard CIA provisions that reflect reasonable and appropriate compliance measures. Doing so is likely to be interpreted as a sign that the organization doesn't get it, and thus needs a more stringent CIA to ensure its compliance.

Organizations also must realize that this is not arm's length negotiating on a level playing field. Obviously, where the OIG conditions a settlement and release from exclusion on a CIA, a company does not have much leverage to take exception with the CIA provisions. However, by carefully picking battles it believes are worth fighting, an organization can focus its attention on convincing the OIG that the alternatives it is proposing are more realistic and just as equally effective as the OIG's approach.

Of course, the OIG should be realistic as well. For example, it cannot expect every physician on the medical staff of a hospital to sit through seven hours of compliance training. Yet, such provisions have been included in CIAs in the past. The problem with such requirements is not only the risk of penalties being imposed for noncompliance, but also the concern that if the standards in the CIA are difficult or impossible to meet, then staff will become skeptical and disheartened by the whole process, which, in the long run, will undermine their commitment to compliance and to the CIA.

## Know What Is Negotiable and What Is Not

A corollary to the need for realistic expectations is the knowledge about which issues may be negotiated. Requirements relating to the basic structure of a compliance plan—such as a compliance officer, a training program, a hotline or other confidential reporting mechanism and written standards of conduct—are not negotiable. However, the areas where the OIG has shown flexibility and, thus, which are more likely to be successfully negotiated, include the following:

▶ *The organizational location of the compliance function within the company and the identification of the personnel who will be responsible for compliance.* This is an area where the OIG will likely be flexible as long as: the compliance officer is a senior executive, senior managers have a defined role in the compliance process and there is an infrastructure in place to support the activities required under the CIA. The OIG will also want to know who the compliance officer reports to, who sits on the compliance committee, whether there is a separate audit committee and how frequently reports are generated for company management regarding compliance issues.

▶ *The content of the training program the company will conduct for all employees and the deadline for conducting that training.* Providers should negotiate the minimum number of hours that make sense for all employees, or for levels of employees. The OIG has demonstrated a willingness to reduce the requirements for general training for all employees, as long as it is balanced by a commitment to provide specialized training for personnel in more sensitive positions, such as billing and marketing.

▶ *The scope of auditing required to be performed by the IRO.* While the OIG generally requires use of its RAT-STATS statistical software for sampling, it has shown great flexibility in defining the scope of work that it expects the IRO to undertake.

It is also important to recognize what is not negotiable so that time is not wasted discussing those issues with the OIG. However, what is nonnegotiable is likely to vary somewhat from case to case. Thus, it is important to test the OIG's flexibility early in the process to determine which issues the organization will likely make the most progress on during negotiations. Below are some of the requirements and areas that do seem beyond negotiation:

▶ Use of an IRO to perform or oversee the auditing activities, and payment for any verification audits by the company

▶ Submission of reports to the OIG, including (1) mandatory disclosure of any overpayments, material deficiencies and government investigations or legal proceedings, and (2) detailed annual reports

▶ Sanction screening requirements for employees and contractors

▶ OIG inspection, audit and review rights

▶ Per diem penalties for violations of the CIA

Regarding this last point, some companies have recently succeeded in convincing the OIG to drop what was once a standard provision that a company could be excluded from Medicare and other federal health care programs if it violated the terms of its CIA.

The term of the CIA, which typically ranges from three to eight years, appears to be a function of the OIG's perception of the seriousness of the misconduct and is generally not subject to extensive negotiation. Where the OIG has required longer-term agreements, it has inserted a somewhat meaningless provision that allows the OIG, at its sole discretion, to reduce the obligations imposed by the CIA after a certain number of years. Under the right circumstances, the OIG may be persuaded to include a provision that would allow the CIA to be terminated short of its full term if the company meets certain criteria.

---

## Use Cost-Benefit Analyses to Justify Proposals

The OIG knows that the compliance department does not have unlimited resources to fully implement the CIA. Since wasteful spending takes away resources from other activities that do yield real compliance benefits, an organization may want to offer alternative proposals along with concrete evidence to support its case, including cost-benefit analyses. If an organization demonstrates that it is motivated by a genuine commitment to compliance, these proposals are much more likely to be seriously considered by the OIG.

## Bring the IRO to the Negotiations

It is a good idea to retain a potential or prospective IRO to assist the company with its CIA negotiations. Including an auditor during negotiations helps the OIG to focus on cost and how to get the most auditing value for the money.

## Closely Review the Requirements for Written Policies and Procedures

The most noteworthy provisions in many recent CIAs have related to the written policies and procedures that the company is required to implement. The OIG appears to be most concerned about accurate coding, medical necessity and aggressive marketing that either generates unnecessary care or involves conduct prohibited by the anti-kickback law. Accept these concerns and work with the OIG to develop appropriate standards. Also, make sure standards parallel existing laws and regulations, and that they do not impose additional requirements that are significantly more burdensome than the rules that apply to the organization's competitors in the industry.

In addition, the standards should be realistic. The OIG has a right to expect that anything that led to wrongdoing will be addressed through revised policies and procedures. For example, the OIG may rightfully be concerned about allowing Medicare to pay for unnecessary care. But if you are a supplier and do not control the ordering physicians, you should not permit yourself to become the guarantor of what they order. If you do, their ordering patterns may result in you being excluded or fined under the CIA. Again, the standards should be consistent with laws and regulations and should not be based on unrealistic expectations, since any failure to conform to the requirements in the CIA could result in fines and exclusion based on the OIG's contractual remedies in the CIA.

## Prepare the First Draft of the IRO Work Plan

Once the OIG presents a company with a first draft of its CIA, the company should develop an audit work plan for the IRO. It is important that the organization—preferably with the assistance of the IRO that eventually will be doing the work—take the initiative to prepare a work plan that addresses all the areas that were the subject of the settlement and is in compliance with the terms of the CIA. A detailed audit work plan, included as part of the CIA, avoids future disagreements about auditing methodologies when the IRO submits its results to the OIG following the first year of the CIA.

In reviewing the organization's proposed work plan, the OIG will be guided by its perception of the wrongdoing that occurred and by its knowledge of the industry's vulnerable areas for fraud, waste and abuse. Obviously, the OIG would like to see all practices and activities audited, while no organization could afford to make that happen. There is room for negotiation to find a comfortable middle ground for both parties. At a minimum, the work plan will need to include statistically valid methodologies so as to permit extrapolation or calculation of an actual overpayment (where the error is systemic and calculation of an actual overpayment is more cost-effective than extrapolation from a sample).

The organization should also try to build into the CIA a gradual transfer of responsibility from the outside IRO to inside auditing staff. The OIG has supported this approach in recent CIAs, which has the dual benefit of saving auditing dollars and building an internal auditing team to take over when the CIA expires.

## Look to Other CIAs for Guidance

Fortunately, negotiating a CIA does not require an organization to reinvent the wheel. The OIG has entered into CIAs with more than 400 health care providers; the overwhelming majority of them have been executed within the past couple of years. These CIAs involve virtually every type of provider, including hospitals, ambulance services, clinical laboratories, home health agencies, hospices, pharmacies, pharmaceutical manufacturers, physician offices, billing services and nursing homes.

Although CIAs are becoming increasingly more detailed, some of the most problematic provisions of past agreements have been remedied in more recent CIAs as the OIG's position continues to evolve.

## Try to Make the OIG a Partner

Finally, organizations should think of the CIA as a partnership with the OIG. The degree of involvement the OIG has regarding how the organization complies with federal program regulations and with the CIA essentially makes the OIG a partner in the company's business. In fact, the OIG is a fairly significant partner, with an array of penalty provisions at its disposal to prove its point.

As with any partnership, the organization runs more smoothly when partners cooperate and trust each other. Therefore, even during the negotiation process the emphasis should be on building trust. Bring the compliance officer to CIA negotiation sessions. Volunteer documents to the OIG to show the effectiveness of the company's current compliance program. If there is a CIA provision that seems unreasonable, try to determine what the OIG's objective is and see if there is another way to achieve it.

As was noted above, it also is important that someone who is familiar with the company and how it does business represent the company during negotiations. Not only does a knowledgeable person help to keep the OIG's expectations realistic, but it is also an opportunity to educate the OIG about the industry and the detailed regulations that already apply to it. This educational process not only results in a better CIA, but it contributes to the building of trust. In other words, the negotiation process should be an opportunity for the company to learn firsthand what the OIG's concerns are and to educate the OIG regarding how those concerns can be addressed most efficiently and effectively.

Remember, the relationship with the OIG does not end with a signed CIA. Rather, the CIA is merely the foundation on which a long-term relationship with the OIG will be built.

# CHAPTER 9

# Preparing for an Independent Review Organization Engagement

## Susan Lemanski

The Office of Inspector General (OIG) of the United States Department of Health and Human Services (DHHS) generally imposes compliance obligations as part of any global resolution of its federal health care program investigations. These compliance obligations typically appear in the form of a corporate integrity agreement (CIA). Government investigations may arise under a variety of civil and criminal false claims statutes, as well as the Civil Monetary Penalties Law. A provider consents to these obligations in exchange for the OIG's release of its authorities to permissively exclude a provider from Medicare, Medicaid and/or other federal health care programs.

Over the past five years, CIAs have undergone dramatic transformations. Most agreements are now 45 pages in length and contain a wide variety of provisions, including detailed requirements related to the federal sentencing guidelines. Most CIAs also contain a provision that requires an entity or individual to obtain and engage an Independent Review Organization (IRO) to perform certain specified procedures related to the entity's or the individual's compliance with the agreement and the accuracy of its claims submissions to the federal health care programs.

As with any independent analysis of an entity's activities, considerable anxiety exists over the type of procedures that will be conducted and the presentation of findings and recommendations to the government. This chapter addresses and clarifies some of the concepts associated with performed procedures under American Institute of Certified Public Accounting (AICPA) standards.

The main issues that an entity faces in preparing for an IRO engagement pursuant to a CIA are: (1) choosing an IRO, (2) defining independence of that IRO, (3) differentiating the audit terminology in the compliance engagement from the billing engagement, (4) developing a mechanism for meeting the time frames in the CIA and (5) discerning the differences in responsibilities under an Agreed-Upon Procedures engagement versus a Consulting engagement. This article discusses each of these challenges and provides guidance on how to reduce the apprehension that inevitably accompanies an audit.

## Independent Review Organizations

Perhaps the first and foremost question that needs to be addressed when preparing for an IRO engagement is, "What is an IRO?" While this appears to be a rather straightforward question, the term "independent review organization" has been the subject of many different interpretations. In addition, as CIAs have evolved, much debate has occurred over the definition of independence for purposes of the IRO. Because the CIAs signed recently by the OIG have generally placed the burden of defining independence on the entity entering into the CIA, the first issue an entity must address is, "What is independence?"

### The OIG Definition of Independence

The OIG typically defines an IRO as "an entity, such as an accounting, auditing or consulting firm that performs review procedures to assist the client in assessing the adequacy of its compliance practices pursuant to this CIA or the applicable contract."[1]  In response to a considerable number of questions regarding what would constitute independence, the OIG has stated that:

> A determination of whether a particular entity, such as a CPA firm, is "independent" for purposes of serving as an IRO is fact specific. At the time of contracting with the IRO, the provider will be in a better position than the OIG to assess the independence of the potential IRO. However, the OIG will consider the IRO's independence when assessing the annual reports and supporting materials by the provider. Factors that raise questions regarding the entity's independence are similar to those cited in the American Institute of Certified Public Accountant's Code of Conduct and SEC rulings. Several of the factors the OIG will consider when assessing an IRO's independence are:
>
> ▶ Whether the IRO or any of its members have a financial interest in the provider
> ▶ Whether the IRO will audit the implementation of a compliance program that it created and implemented for the provider
> ▶ Whether and to what extent the IRO was involved in the provider's management decisions (including, for example, reporting to the Board of Directors, fielding hotline calls, appointing the compliance officer or determining the content of training)
> ▶ Whether the IRO played any role in operating the provider's compliance program[2]

The OIG further stated that "if a provider has a concern over the appearance of a lack of independence, it should carefully analyze whether that IRO can in fact provide its services in an independent manner."[3] This presents the entity with its first challenge in preparing for an IRO engagement—selecting an IRO. The OIG's response places the onus of determining independence on the entity operating under the CIA.

**AICPA independence standards.**  Because the OIG points to the AICPA and the Securities and Exchange Commission (SEC) for additional guidance on independence, an entity should consult both the AICPA's definition of independence and the SEC's recent guidance

---

1. The excerpt is from the OIG's "Frequently Asked Questions Related to OIG Corporate Integrity Agreements," available at http://oig.hhs.gov/ciafaq1.htm.

2. *Ibid.*

3. *Ibid.*

on independence. "The AICPA has established through its Code of Professional Conduct, precepts to guard against the presumption of a loss of independence.'Presumption' is stressed because the possession of intrinsic independence is a matter of personal quality rather than rules that formulate certain objectives tests. Insofar as these precepts have been incorporated into the profession's code, they have the force of professional law for the independent auditor."[4]

In notes to the Interpretation of Rule 101 on Independence, the AICPA states that "independence shall be considered impaired, if for example, a member had any of the following transactions, interests or relationships:

▶ During the period of a professional engagement or at the time of expressing an opinion, a member or a member's firm:
  – Had or was committed to acquire any direct or material indirect financial interest in the enterprise.
  – Was a trustee of any trust or executor or administrator of any estate if such trust or estate had or was committed to acquire any direct or material indirect financial interest in the enterprise.
  – Had any joint, closely held business investment with the enterprise or with any officer, director, or principal stockholders thereof that was material in relation to the member's net worth or to the net worth of the member's firm.
  – Had any loan to or from the enterprise or any officer, director or principal stockholder of the enterprise except as specifically permitted in interpretation 101–5.
▶ During the period covered by the financial statements, during the period of the professional engagement, or at the time of expressing an opinion, a member or a member's firm:
  – Was connected with the enterprise as a promoter, underwriter or voting trustee, as a director, officer, or employee, or in any capacity equivalent to that of a member of management.
  – Was a trustee for any pension or profit-sharing trust of the enterprise."[5]

The AICPA has further defined independence in an attestation engagement[6] to mean "the objective consideration of facts, unbiased judgments, and honest neutrality on the part of the practitioner in forming and expressing conclusions. It implies not the attitude of a prosecutor, but the judicial impartiality that recognizes an obligation of fairness."[7] Compliance engagements are conducted pursuant to Statement of Position 99-1, which established the procedures for performing an Agreed-Upon Procedures engagement pursuant to a CIA. Agreed-Upon Procedures are attestation engagements, and thus are subject to the additional independence requirements articulated above.

---

4. See AICPA's *Codification of Statements on Auditing Standards*, AU Section 220.04.

5. See AICPA Rule 101.02. Paragraph added by adoption of the Code of Professional Conduct on January 12, 1988. Revised, effective June 30, 1990, by the Professional Ethics Executive Committee. Revised, November 1991, effective January 1, 1992 with earlier application encouraged, by the Professional Ethics Executive Committee. Revised, effective February 28, 1998, by the Professional Ethics Executive Committee.

6. Under the AICPA's *Codification of Statements on Auditing Standards*, AT Section 100.01, an "attest engagement" is one in which a practitioner is engaged to issue or does issue written communication that expresses a conclusion about the reliability of a written assertion that is the responsibility of another party. An "assertion" is any declaration, or set of related declarations taken as a whole, by a party responsible for it.

7. See AT Section 100.27.

It should be noted that the AICPA states that the examples given above are not intended to be all inclusive. It is part of the practitioner's responsibility and, in this case, the responsibility of the entity operating under the CIA, to evaluate the facts and circumstances in making a determination of independence.

The AICPA's guidance also addresses the time frame for which independence is implicated. The guidance states, "The period of a professional engagement starts when the member begins to perform any professional services requiring independence for an enterprise, lasts for the entire duration of the professional relationship, which could cover many periods, and ends with the formal or informal notification of the termination of the professional relationship either by the member, by the enterprise, or by the issuance of a report, whichever is later. Accordingly, the professional engagement does not end with the issuance of a report and recommence with the signing of the following year's engagement."[8]

**SEC independence standards.**   Because the OIG has also referred to the SEC in its statements on independence, it is important to consider the recently released guidance from the SEC. On November 15, 2000, the SEC released *The Commission's Proposal to Modernize the Rules Governing the Independence of the Accounting Profession*. In its press release, the SEC stated that "the commission will consider the adoption of rules that modernize the requirements for auditor independence in three areas: (1) investments by auditors and their family members in audit clients; (2) employment relationships between auditors or their family members and audit clients; and (3) scope of services provided by audit firms to their audit clients."[9]

**Evaluating an IRO's independence.**   To evaluate independence of a potential IRO, the entity under the CIA should consider two types of arrangements. First, the entity should evaluate any ownership arrangements or joint ventures that the IRO has with the entity. Certified Public Accountants (CPAs) are required to track ownership interests in their financial audit clients and this information is helpful in evaluating independence issues in the context of an IRO engagement.

In addition to evaluating an IRO's potential financial relationships, the entity should also consider the IRO's involvement in the management process. In particular, if the IRO has assumed a managerial role with decision-making authority in the entity, the IRO's independence may be questioned.

**Time frame for selecting an IRO.**   The typical CIA contains provisions that require the entity under the CIA to select an IRO within 120 days of the effective date of the CIA.[10] The entity also has to report to the OIG the name of the IRO, as well as the dates of initiation and completion of the IRO engagement(s). The earlier an IRO is engaged in the implementation of the CIA, the more likely the entity will be prepared for the IRO's engagement(s).

---

8. *Ibid.*

9. See The Commission's "Proposal to Modernize the Rules Governing the Independence of the Accounting Profession," available at http://www.sec.gov/news/extra/faqaud.htm.

10. The "effective date" of a CIA is generally defined as the date on which the last signature on the CIA was obtained.

## Independent Review Organization Engagements

Generally, CIAs involve two separate and distinct engagements. While this is dependent on a variety of factors, including the type of entity entering into the CIA, the typical CIA contains provisions for both a compliance engagement and a billing engagement. Differentiating between these engagements is important because the entity entering into a CIA has different responsibilities under each of these engagements.

The compliance engagement is generally formulated as an Agreed-Upon Procedures engagement, which is an attestation[11] engagement under AICPA standards.[12] "An *attest engagement* is one in which a practitioner is engaged to issue or does issue written communication that expresses a conclusion about the reliability of a written assertion that is the responsibility of another party."[13] An assertion is any declaration, or set of related declarations taken as a whole, by a party responsible for it.[14] In the context of a compliance engagement, the IRO is testing management's assertions regarding its compliance with the CIA or the integrity provisions in the Settlement Agreement entered into between the entity and the OIG. An Agreed-Upon Procedures engagement requires the IRO to present specific findings to assist the users[15] in evaluating management's assertion about an entity's compliance with specified requirements. Because the OIG and the entity will be users of the report, both will be involved in formulating the procedures to be used to test the entity's compliance with the CIA. As part of the planning process, the IRO should circulate procedures to both the entity and the OIG to obtain agreement regarding the procedures to be performed.

In contrast, the billing engagement is typically conducted in accordance with consulting standards. Consulting standards are generally more loosely defined and more subjective in nature.. The reason a billing engagement is usually conducted pursuant to a Consulting Procedures engagement (as opposed to an Agreed-Upon Procedures engagement) is that the billing engagement generally requires subjective evaluations; in contrast, Agreed-Upon Procedures engagements must be formulated in response to objective criteria.[16] The evaluation of an entity's billing requires the inherent use of judgment. As such, it would be impossible to formulate procedures that would allow two equally qualified individuals to reach the same coding conclusion in every instance.

---

11. Under the AICPA's *Codification of Statements on Auditing Standards,* AT Section 100.01, an "attest engagement" is one in which a practitioner is engaged to issue or does issue written communication that expresses a conclusion about the reliability of a written assertion that is the responsibility of another party. An "assertion" is any declaration, or set of related declarations taken as a whole, by a party responsible for it.

12. The AICPA issued a Statement of Position on May xx, 1999 entitled "Guidance on Conducting Agreed-Upon Procedures for Corporate Integrity Agreements," SOP 99-1.

13. *Ibid.*

14. See also, AICPA's "Statements for Standards for Attestation Engagements," No. 9.

15. "Users" of the compliance engagement would be defined as the OIG and the entity that engaged the IRO to perform these procedures. In certain circumstances, the CIA contains multiple addressees of the report. Unless subsequent agreements have been reached, each addressee would be considered a user of the report.

16. See AICPA's *Codification of Statements on Auditing Standards,* AT 500A.25.

## Timeline of a Typical IRO Engagement

In preparing for an IRO, it is important to realize that the engagement time frame is usually at least a year. The typical CIA requires the IRO to evaluate the entity for at least one year after the effective date of the CIA. Generally, an IRO will issue its report(s) approximately two months after the close of the established review period. Throughout this 14-month period, the IRO and the entity should set deadlines to facilitate the timely completion of the IRO's engagement. There are usually four phases of an IRO engagement: (1) the planning stage; (2) the fieldwork; (3) the report generation; and (4) the response to the IRO's report. See Table 1, a typical timeline for an IRO engagement.

### Table 1.  Typical Timeline for an IRO Engagement

| Event | Proposed Date |
|---|---|
| Sign CIA | January 1, 2001 |
| Engage IRO | March 1, 2001 |
| Submit Implementation Report | April 1, 2001 |
| First draft of IRO work plans | April 1, 2001 |
| Refine IRO work plans | May 16, 2001 |
| IRO submits work plans to the OIG for agreement | June 1, 2001 |
| IRO submits draft data request for both the billing engagement and the compliance engagement | June 15, 2001 |
| Proposed kick-off meeting | June 25, 2001 |
| XYZ provides IRO with sample universe of claims | February 25, 2002 |
| IRO selects probe sample from claims listing above and returns sample selection (encounter and enrollment data) | March 1, 2002 |
| XYZ photocopies and sends data related to each of 30 selected line items (see client assistance list) for its analysis of the probe sample | March, 10 2002 |
| IRO completes analysis of probe sample and compiles results | March 17, 2002 |
| IRO conducts statistical analysis to determine full sample size and selects sample units | March 20, 2002 |
| XYZ receives sample selection and copies pertinent portions of the medical records for those line items selected | March 27, 2002 |
| Beginning of annual IRO field work for both the billing engagement and compliance engagement | April 1, 2002 |
| IRO conducts fieldwork on billing engagement and compliance engagement | April 1–15, 2002 |
| IRO begins tabulating results for billing engagement | April 15–20, 2002 |
| IRO begins drafting the annual IRO reports | April 20, 2002 |
| Partner review | April 26–28, 2002 |
| Final IRO report due to XYZ | April 29, 2002 |
| Annual report due to the OIG | May 1, 2002 |

**Planning an IRO engagement.**  The planning phase of the engagement lasts until the IRO obtains agreement from the OIG on the procedures to be performed for the compliance engagement and comments on the billing engagement. This phase concludes once the IRO arrives on site to begin its substantive procedures.

There are several important steps that should occur during the planning stage. First, the IRO and the entity should plan a kick-off meeting to review the workplan(s) together. It is essential that certain key people attend the meeting in order to discuss the exchange of information that will be necessary to complete an IRO engagement. At a minimum, the compliance officer, the director of Internal Audit, the billing supervisor and a representative from Information Systems (who will be pulling the data) should be present at this meeting.

In preparation for the kickoff meeting, the compliance officer and the billing supervisor should carefully read the IRO's proposed workplan(s) and note any deviations from either the CIA or the entity's current practices. The compliance officer and the billing manager should also consider any changes in practice or changes in reimbursement rules since the effective date of the CIA. These changes could have a significant impact on the scope of the engagement or the design of the procedures.

Information systems personnel should pay close attention to the sampling unit required by the CIA and addressed in the workplan. Generally, the OIG requests "paid claims" as the sampling unit. However, determination of the sampling unit will depend on the type of entity involved since not every entity has the ability to capture payment data on a line item basis. The compliance officer should consult with the Information Systems department to determine the appropriate sample unit. Similarly, the information systems personnel should be consulted to consider the statistical sampling methodology required by the CIA or proposed by the IRO. This methodology will drive the format of the data files necessary to complete any random sampling required by the CIA.

In concluding the kickoff meeting, the IRO and the entity should come to consensus regarding timelines for the remainder of the engagement. In addition, the IRO and the entity should designate individuals responsible for obtaining data and supporting documentation, and resolving any ambiguities that exist in the workplans. An effective approach to resolving ambiguities is for the entity to draft a letter to the OIG that requests clarification of any issues in question. This is particularly helpful when there has been a significant change in the reimbursement methods affecting the entity under the CIA.

Based on the discussions that occurred during the kick-off meeting, the entity should have: (1) draft procedures that will be performed pursuant to the IRO engagement(s), (2) a client assistance list that sets forth the responsibilities of the entity in connection with the IRO engagement(s), (3) a tentative timetable for completing the IRO engagement(s), (4) a draft of the letter of management's assertions and (5) a draft of the letter of management's representations.

An especially effective strategy to help an entity to prepare for an IRO is for the entity to take the draft workplans (that have been refined as a result of the kickoff meeting) and perform an internal walk-through of the draft procedures articulated in the workplan. This should provide the entity with a gap analysis of the worksteps that must be accomplished prior to the inception of the IRO's planned procedures. A wide variety of project management tools are available to help the entity close the gap between the procedures and the current practice. In addition, several software companies have developed project management tools that can help a compliance officer formulate action plans to respond to the requirements of a CIA.

As the inception of the IRO engagement nears, the IRO and the entity should begin to have frequent, scheduled communication. Approximately two months before fieldwork is to begin, the IRO and the entity should begin having weekly conference calls. These calls facilitate direct and clear communication of expectations and ensure proper transmission of information.

**Fieldwork.**  Generally, an IRO is on site for approximately two weeks, although this is entirely dependent upon the sample size, as determined by the probe sample, and can vary greatly according to the CIA. It should also be noted that the OIG has allowed interim testing[17] and the use of Internal Audit. If the entity's CIA contains either of these provisions, the sample size, as well as the time frame needed to complete the on-site procedures, could be significantly reduced.

As a part of the fieldwork, the compliance officer and the billing manager should have the materials requested by the IRO available upon the IRO's arrival on site. In addition, both of these individuals should be accessible for interviews with the IRO to discuss the operations of their respective departments and to clarify any ambiguities in the documentation.

Upon the close of fieldwork, the IRO generally will present preliminary findings in the form of an exit interview.

**Report generation.**  Once the fieldwork is complete, the IRO usually begins drafting its reports; a draft report takes, on average, approximately two weeks to complete. Generally, by the time the draft report is completed and forwarded to the entity for its review, the IRO will have requested a Letter of Management's Assertions and a Letter of Management's Representations.

The typical CIA engagement allows approximately one week for management's review of the draft report before it must be finalized for dissemination to the OIG.

**Response to the report.**  The OIG typically requires the entity to respond to the findings from the IRO's report in its annual report. Because the IRO's report and the entity's response must be produced simultaneously, the timely exchange of information during this time frame is particularly important. In addition to any subjective corrective action plans the entity plans to implement in response to the IRO's findings, the entity is required to submit any overpayments, pursuant to the IRO's billing engagement, back to the appropriate payor. More recent CIAs have included an overpayment form as an attachment to the CIA. Nonetheless, all entities operating under a CIA should have received correspondence from the OIG communicating this requirement.

## Preparing for the Independent Review Organization

### Compliance engagement

1. **Responsibility for Procedures.**  In preparing for the IRO engagement, it is important to recognize that while the compliance and billing engagements occur virtually simultaneously, the responsibilities of the entity under the compliance engagement are different. As a specified user in an Agreed-Upon Procedures engagement, the entity accepts responsibility for the adequacy and sufficiency of the procedures. This means the entity should be an active participant in formulating these procedures and, as required by AICPA guidance, will be required to affirmatively agree to the procedures.[18] While the procedures designed to test compliance with this agreement

---

17. Generally, interim testing is conducted semiannually or quarterly.

18. To satisfy the requirements that the IRO and the specified users agree upon the procedures performed or to be performed, and that the specified users take responsibility for the sufficiency of the agreed-upon procedures for their purposes, ordinarily the practitioner should communicate directly with and obtain affirmative acknowledgment from each of the specified users. See AICPA's *Codification of Statements on Auditing Standards*, AT 500A.17.

should place no additional burden on the entity beyond the requirements of the CIA, the entity should thoroughly review the proposed procedures to ascertain whether they accurately evaluate the requirements of the CIA. Once the procedures have been agreed to by the entity, they should be formalized and sent to the OIG for its review and approval.

2. **Problem areas for the Agreed-Upon Procedures Engagement.** There are two main problems that entities often face in preparing for an IRO engagement: (1) documenting the entity's compliance with the required provisions and (2) creating information systems to support the documentation. To alleviate these problems, the entity should begin with the end in mind, considering that for each of the requirements of the CIA, the entity will have to provide the IRO, and perhaps ultimately the OIG, with documentation of compliance with each particular requirement.

One of the most useful tools to ensure that documentation exists, and that a requirement has been completed on a timely basis, is a timetable (Table 2). This quick checklist is designed to keep the compliance officer focused on the numerous deadlines that are an essential part of every CIA. In addition to the timetable, the compliance officer should establish a centralized source for tracking these reporting requirements. Generally, assigning this responsibility to a project manager who will be able to track progress and keep the organization focused on the next impending deadline helps to ensure that all requirements are completed on time.

Many of these requirements and deadlines impact other areas of the organization; therefore, it is important to delegate responsibility for specific activities to specific departments early on in the process. For example, the department that typically takes the responsibility to screen for "ineligible persons" is Human Resources. While the compliance officer may rely on Human Resources documentation to show that every individual has been checked against the OIG and General Services Administration (GSA) lists, ultimately it is the compliance officer who must certify that this has been done within the prescribed time frames. Therefore, the compliance officer must be involved in the process for monitoring the progress of this requirement. For any requirement that has been delegated to another department, the compliance officer may want to select and test small samples to provide reasonable assurance that the responsible department is carrying out its delegated activities.

There are primarily four areas of vulnerability that compliance officers should be aware of when establishing documentation protocols pursuant to the requirements of a CIA. These are areas in which entities operating under CIAs typically receive findings in the compliance report. They include problems with (1) documentation of the distribution of the code of conduct, (2) documentation of the certifications for general and specific employee training, (3) documentation that each covered person has been checked against the OIG and GSA lists to identify ineligible persons and (4) documentation that overpayments have been returned to the appropriate payor. While completing these tasks pursuant to the time frames is challenging, maintaining documentation creates additional challenges that can be nearly insurmountable without the use of electronic databases.

It should be noted that three of the four problems listed above focus on tracking the activities of a large number of people. It should also be noted that there is not a date certain for when these activities need to be completed. For example, new "covered persons" typically need to be trained within 120 days of employment; however, there are different deadlines for "currently" covered people and for "new" covered people.

Another challenge posed by the maintenance of this documentation is keeping track of individuals known as "covered persons" (e.g., vendors, contractors). While the entity probably already has an established database of employed individuals, it is

## Table 2.  Sample CIA Timeline

| Days Due After Effective Date of CIA | Calendar Date | Requirement | Completed |
|---|---|---|---|
| 90 days | 4.20.00 | Distribute Code of Conduct to all employees, contractors or agents | |
| 90 days | 4.20.00 | Develop and implement written policies and procedures regarding the compliance program (1) proper billing procedures for inpatient stays and outpatient services (2) inpatient claims with a bill type be subject to a pre-billing review (3) disciplinary guidelines and methods to make disclosures. | |
| | 4.20.00 | The relevant portions of the policies and procedures shall be distributed to all appropriate employees, contractors and/or agents. | |
| 90 days | 4.20.00 | General training has been provided to all employees, contractors and agents. | |
| 90 days | 4.20.00 | Specific training has been provided to each employee, contractor and/or agent who is involved directly or indirectly in the preparation. | |
| 90 days | 4.20.00 | Obtain certifications from each employee that they have attended general and specific training. | |
| 90 days | 4.20.00 | XYZ has established its internal review group or retained an Independent Review Organization to perform procedures to assist in assessing the adequacy of its inpatient and outpatient billings. | |
| 120 days | 5.20.00 | Obtain certifications on the Code of Conduct from employees, contractor and/or agent | |
| | 5.20.00 | Implementation Report is due at the OIG. This report shall include: (1) the name, address, phone number, and position description of the Compliance Officer; | |

| Days Due After Effective Date of CIA | Calendar Date | Requirement | Completed |
|---|---|---|---|
| | | (2) the names and positions of the members of the Compliance Committee;<br>(3) copy of the Medical Center's Code of Conduct;<br>(4) summary of the policies and procedures;<br>(5) a description of the training program, including a description of the targeted audiences and a schedule of when training sessions were held;<br>(6) a certification by the compliance officer that: policies have been completed and distributed, Code of Conduct certification is complete, training certifications have been executed<br>(7) a description of the confidential disclosure program;<br>(8) the identity of the IRO and proposed start and complete dates;<br>(9) summary of personnel actions taken; also the certification requirements in section IV.C. | |
| 121 days | 5.22.00 | Begin developing audit work plan. Establish universe of claims, attributes of sample, and sampling approach. This may include stratification of the population. | |
| 180 days | 7.20.00 | Prepare and submit work plan to the OIG. (See SOP 99-1). The OIG must have at least 90 days to review an audit work plan. In order to begin fieldwork, this work plan must be submitted to the OIG for comment at least 150 days prior to field work start date. | |
| 1 year and 3 days | 02.20.01 | Annual report is due at the OIG. | |

*Source:* Ernst & Young LLP. Reproduced with permission.

unlikely that it has established a database that also tracks "covered individuals." As a result, the entity will have to identify those individuals it defines as covered individuals and develop a method, with the assistance of operational personnel, for keeping track of when the entity contracts with these individuals. This communication must occur rather rapidly because the deadlines for training and distribution of the code of conduct occur generally within 120 days of execution of the individual contract in question.

The last problem listed above—documenting return of overpayments to payors—usually involves the Accounts Payable department. The return of overpayments is typically an item that is overlooked in the initial implementation of the CIA; as a result, very often there are no established methods of documenting the return of these overpayments.

3. **Preparing for the Agreed-Upon Procedures Engagement.** Approximately one month prior to the IRO engagement, the compliance officer should determine if the IRO has obtained agreement to the procedures from the OIG. If such agreement has been obtained, the compliance officer should begin to collect the information that will be required pursuant to the client assistance list. Some of the information required on the list will likely come from other departments within the organization. Therefore, the earlier the compliance officer can inform these departments about the information that will be requested of them, the more likely the information will be provided in an organized, timely manner.

IRO compliance procedures are typically organized in the order of the CIA, and requested materials should be organized with that in mind. This should reduce the amount of time required to complete the procedures and also reduce the number of inquiries directed at the compliance officer. Furthermore, the procedures will include an interview with the compliance officer and his or her designees. This interview usually addresses any areas of the CIA for which the organization does not have written documentation, such as how the confidential disclosure program works and how the code of conduct was disseminated. The interview will also cover any requirements of the CIA for which the entity lacks complete documentation.

4. **Form of the Agreed-Upon Procedures Report.** The Independent Accountant's Report of Agreed-Upon Procedures will consist of:

   a. Identification of the specified users.
   b. A reference to, or statement of, management's assertion about the entity's compliance with specified requirements.
   c. A list of the procedures performed.
   d. A statement that the practitioner was not engaged to, and did not perform, an examination of management's assertion about compliance with the specified requirements or about the effectiveness of an entity's internal control over compliance.
   e. Findings pursuant to the procedures performed.[19]

For purposes of compliance with a CIA, the IRO should require specific assertions regarding each of the sections of the CIA. For example, one of the management's assertions that an IRO will require is that the entity appoint a compliance officer within 120 days of the effective date of the CIA.[20]

---

19. See AICPA's *Codification of Statements on Auditing Standards*, AT 500A.23.

20. For additional management's assertions pertaining to an IRO's compliance engagement, see AICPA's Statement of Position, 99-1.

Although the letter of management's written representations is not included as part of the report, it should be obtained prior to issuance of the report. Among the representations that should be included in the letter of management's written representations are:

a. An acknowledgment of management's responsibility for complying with the CIA.
b. An acknowledgment of management's responsibility for establishing and maintaining effective control over compliance.
c. A statement that management has made all documentation related to the specified requirements.
d. A statement that management has disclosed any communications from regulatory agencies, internal auditors and other practitioners concerning possible noncompliance with the specified requirements.
e. A statement of management's interpretation of any compliance requirements that have varying interpretations.[21]

Management's refusal to furnish all appropriate written representations constitutes a limitation on the scope of the engagement that requires the practitioner to withdraw from the engagement.

## Billing Engagement

1. **Responsibility for Procedures.**  Whereas the OIG is a specified user of the compliance engagement, the OIG generally does not take responsibility for the sufficiency and adequacy of the billing procedures. As such, it is important that the entity and the IRO regularly communicate regarding the consulting procedures to be performed in response to the requirements under the billing engagement. Although the OIG takes no responsibility under the standards of a consulting engagement, both the entity and the IRO have knowledge that the OIG will be a user of the report. Therefore, if the CIA contains requirements that are not well defined, it is important for the IRO and the entity to obtain clarification from the OIG on the parameters of the engagement. The billing engagement generally consists of at least two parts: (1) a claims analysis and (2) cost report procedures that typically address unallowable costs pursuant to the Settlement Agreement.

2. **Problem areas for the Agreed-Upon Procedures Engagements.**  The issues most often encountered during the billing engagement have to do with information systems and the statistical sampling parameters as set forth in the CIA. For example, an entity entering into a CIA should evaluate its ability to pull data in a format that would allow selection of a random sample in accordance with the parameters set forth in the CIA. An entity should also evaluate, early in the implementation of a CIA, its ability to track payment data in its current accounts receivable system. This is important because the most recent CIAs have required an entity to select a statistically valid random sample of paid claims. Another significant issue is the unpredictability of the sample size. The IRO's sample size is driven by a variety of factors, including the error rate of the probe sample as well as the homogeneity of the errors in the probe sample. Because these factors are not predictable, it is impossible to know at the beginning of the year precisely the amount of resources that will need to be devoted to the claims analysis.

---

21. See AICPA's *Codification of Statements on Auditing Standards*, AT 500.70.

The billing engagement also typically contains provisions requiring the IRO to assess the entity's cost report for certain unallowable costs pursuant to the Settlement Agreement. These unallowable costs are generally defined as:

a. Costs incurred on behalf of the entity pertaining to the matters covered in the Settlement Agreement.
b. Costs incurred on behalf of the entity in connection with the government's civil and criminal investigation, including attorney's fees, or the CIA.
c. The entity's investigation, defense or corrective actions taken in response to the government's civil and criminal investigation.
d. The negotiation of the Settlement Agreement or the CIA.
e. Payment made pursuant to the Settlement Agreement.

The more recent CIAs require the entity to identify to the IRO any unallowable costs that have been included in payments sought in cost reports or cost statements. Obviously, the list of unallowable costs will be more readily available and easier to compile the closer this is done to the effective date of the CIA. As such, the compliance officer should communicate this requirement to the reimbursement personnel responsible for the submission of any cost report or cost statement submitted to the federal government.

**3. Form of the Agreed-Upon Report.** Unlike the Agreed-Upon Procedures report, which has a very specific format, a consulting report can take on a variety of formats. *However, the OIG has recently released guidance that specifies the format that the IRO should use in submitting a billing engagement report.*

---

## Conclusion

One of the key ingredients of a successful IRO engagement is to begin the planning process early. In fact, the IRO engagements that run most effectively are often those in which the planning began prior to the signing of the CIA. It is important to remember that many of these engagements require significant changes in an organization's information systems and operations. As such, preparing for an IRO engagement early in the process and communicating with the appropriate operations personnel are essential to the success of any IRO engagement.

# Glossary

| | |
|---|---|
| ABA | American Bar Association |
| AICPA | American Institute of Certified Public Accounting |
| ALJ | Administrative Law Judge |
| CCO | Chief Compliance Officer |
| CEO | Chief Executive Officer |
| CFO | Chief Financial Officer |
| CIA | Corporate Integrity Agreement |
| CMP | Civil Monetary Penalties |
| CMPL | Civil Monetary Penalties Law |
| CMS | Centers for Medicare and Medicaid Services |
| COO | Chief Operating Officer |
| CPA | Certified Public Accountant |
| DHHS | Department of Health and Human Services |
| DMEPOS | Durable Medical Equipment, Prosthetic and Orthotic Suppliers |
| DOJ | Department of Justice |
| EPA | Environmental Protection Agency |
| GAO | General Accounting Office |
| GASP | Generally Accepted Statistical Procedures |
| GSA | General Services Administration |
| HCFA | Health Care Financing Administration |
| HIPAA | Health Insurance Portability and Accountability Act |
| IRO | Independent Review Organization |
| JCAHO | Joint Commission on Accreditation of Healthcare Organizations |
| MAC | Medicare Appeals Council (of the Department of Health and Human Services' Departmental Appeals Board) |
| MCM | Medicare Carriers Manual |
| MIM | Medicare Intermediary Manual |
| OIG | Office of Inspector General |
| PCG | Public Consulting Group |
| RFP | Request for Proposals |
| SEC | U.S. Securities and Exchange Commission |
| SUR | Surveillance and Utilization Control units |